HERDMATES TO HEARTMATES:

The Art of Bonding with a New Horse

Published in the United States by BookLocker.com, Inc., Port Charlotte, Florida.

Printed in the United States of America on acid-free paper.

Bonnie Ebsen Jackson
www.t-h-e.ranch.com
P.O. Box 256
Skull Valley, AZ 86338
2012

First Edition

HERDMATES TO HEARTMATES:

The Art of Bonding with a New Horse

Bonnie Ebsen Jackson

Dedications

To all the new horses I have ever owned—especially those that came with secrets to learn and problems to solve.

To my husband Bruce and son John, who never gave up on me or, if they did, never let on.

To my students and clients, from my teachers and mentors, for that is the flow...

Acknowledgements

Thanks to my parents for screwing me up just enough to make my life interesting and my soul hungry to write a book in the first place (Just kidding...actually, I'd like to thank my father for constantly reminding me, "Bonnie, you're a writer; you should write.")

Thanks to my sister Kiki for continually raising the bar on so many levels.

Thanks to my posse of "horsy" friends, new and old, near and far—Allena, Dora, Heather, Jessica, Sharon, Mary & Tom, Sue & John, Lisa, Terry, Shannon, Rich, Alison, Deborah Sue, and Alec—all of us connected through our love of the magical beasts we ride.

Thank you Linda at Richey Design for your abundant talent and patience.

Thank you H. Knowles, for using your OCD super powers for good and delivering some wicked mad last minute editing. You rock!

Special thanks to Reg Saybrook, whose work with wild horse herds led him to create the exercise I refer to in this book as "Follow Me."

Thanks to Zack and Zoë for your, ahem, help with the horses.

About the Author - Bonnie Ebsen Jackson

There is a photo of Bonnie at age three, sitting astride a massive white horse on a windy beach in Baja California. Hair haloed around her face, she peers at the camera with a look of rapture tinged with annoyance as she gestures at the lead rope in the hands of an unseen adult. Without question, her message is, "Let me loose, NOW! I want to RIDE this bad boy!" That is possibly all you need to know about Bonnie and her lifelong love affair with all things equine.

Raised on a 35-acre ranch just a half-hour commute from Hollywood, California (her dad was television actor Buddy Ebsen), Bonnie spent her youth training and showing horses before being bitten by the acting bug herself. The bite did not prove fatal, however, and Bonnie eventually transitioned back to the horse world, writing and editing for two different horse publications. Ultimately, Bonnie would combine her passion for horses with her passion to help others heal and improve their lives through equine-assisted experiential education and psychotherapy.

Today, Bonnie owns and operates T.H.E. Ranch (Teaching Humans with Equine)™ just outside Prescott, Arizona. The ranch offers experiential education and psychotherapy, "Life Skills" natural horsemanship, and relational riding, along with coaching for new and struggling horse owners. She will often host special topic women's support retreats and corporate trainings at the ranch, where she and her husband Bruce offer waterfront guest accommodations. For more information on T.H.E. Ranch and its activities, email Bonnie@t-h-e-ranch.com.

Table of Contents

Introduction: Your Horse is Not a Mountain Bike

"A horse is the projection of peoples' dreams about themselves—strong, powerful, beautiful—and it has the capability of giving us escape from our mundane existence."—Pam Brown

"Horses can't talk but they can speak if you listen."—Anon.

Have you ever bought a mountain bike? You see the bike in the store, all bright and shiny and new, and you buy it. You take the bike home, set it in a corner, still shiny and new. Every once in a while, you take it for a ride up that pretty mountain trail with all the scenic views. At those times, you are at one with the bike, working all its gears and zooming down the straight-aways. Then you bring it home, wipe it down until it's

1

bright and shiny again, and put it back in its corner until the next ride.

Although they may both go down the same mountain trails, a horse and a mountain bike are not the same.

To illustrate what I mean, contrast the above scenario with this one:

You see the horse of your dreams at the sale barn, all freshly bathed and shiny, and being put through its paces in a calm and relaxed way. What a beautiful horse! What fun it would be to own and ride that horse! You buy and bring the horse to its new home. Suddenly, the once calm and steady mount you rode at the sale barn is replaced by a prancing, lathered, beast of the Apocalypse, with doomed and hollow eyes. Still, you now own your dream horse and you can't wait for your first ride together. On the first nice day, you race to the stable all set to saddle up and ride your shiny new horse on that pretty trail with all the scenic views. You arrive at his stall only to find that he's had a dust-up with his neighbor overnight and is now sporting a huge bite mark on his withers, where the saddle goes; a deep oozing sore where his back leg kicked at the fence panels in retaliation; and, to top it off, he's missing the shoe on that hoof.

Once the vet and farrier have been called and he's been put back together, you saddle up and go for that long anticipated ride on your new horse. More like "Mr. Toad's Wild Ride," as your mount executes a series of swerves from horse "monsters" that appear much larger in his brain than in real life. He alternates between spurts of adrenaline-fueled speed, during which the bridle reins seem to have the efficacy of Maypole ribbons, and short pauses to mow the grass by the side of the road. Finally, you slip off and trudge back home, wishing your new horse had come with an operator's manual.

Believe it or not, this horse really wants to connect with you, to be the well-behaved mount you rode at the sale barn. The problem is that he's a sentient being, a prey animal that needs to be reassured he's not all alone in his quest for survival. With the change of ownership, what used to give him assurance, comfort, and companionship has now changed. Without the familiar sights and sounds of his old environment, he has no idea where he stands in the "food chain existence" that is the life of any prey animal. For instance, he used to know every inch of his home territory—vastly important in figuring out from where the tigers and bears will emerge. Now, he's in a new stable, possibly confined to just a box stall with no view of his surroundings. The adjacent horse is unfriendly, or worse, he might not have a neighbor at all! You come to his stall with halter in hand, but you look different, smell different, and sound different from his last owner. In short, you don't really register with him yet; he has absolutely no confidence that you have his best interests at heart or are resourceful enough to keep him safe when predators come calling.

The good news is that while your horse may never be as convenient as your mountain bike, he can become just as enjoyable if the two of you can learn a common language. Since *his* knowledge of spoken language will be mostly limited to words like "whoa," "cookie," and commands to walk, trot and canter, communication can improve vastly when you begin to tune into what your horse is saying with his body. Learning to read your horse's behavior and understand his needs will eventually help you to decipher all horses' behavior.

Having a sentient being for transportation can have its advantages; while a mountain bike will never alert you to a cougar lurking in the bushes, your equine partner will give you plenty of warning, which might just save your life!

Why You Should Read *This* Book

When I first started to write a book, I thought about all the books on horse care, horse behavior, and horse training that already existed and wondered what would make mine different. What did I have to say, and to whom exactly did I want to say it?

In reality, there are trainers, clinicians, "gurus" and "whisperers," who have covered a great deal of how-to horse information. It is quite nearly information overload for someone who is new to horses! Because new horse owners, future owners, and those who are just getting interested in horses are in the reader audience I want to address, I decided to present a more personal account of what I've learned about getting to know a variety of new horses. This gives me the freedom to speak my mind from my own experience. Others might have different experiences that brought them to different conclusions on the topics covered here. As we say in experiential education, telling your story "is what it is" and no one can dispute your telling of it. Saying that, I have taken great pains not to lead anyone too far astray in my ruminations, advice, and suggestions.

Much of what I say is informed not just by my experience as a horse owner and enthusiast, but also as a horse professional for the last two decades. Thus far, my experience has covered:

- Horse magazine writer/editor
- Boarding facility manager
- Trail ride outfitter
- Riding instructor
- Life skills horsemanship teacher for at-risk youth
- Equine-assisted mental health facilitator.

The constant theme through most of these occupations is, of course, gathering and communicating useful information about the horse. In most of them, I've had a chance to update my knowledge, skills and procedures through the experience of others and my own hands-on experiences. You see, I'm still a student at heart and always will be.

Your new horse, or the horse you will be getting sometime in the near future, will not care if you read this book from cover to cover (but I heartily recommend you do so) as long as you get its message. Your new horse is mainly interested in how skilled and knowledgeable you are as a fellow herd member. That's right—

you will be seen first as a predator, then as a friendly predator, and finally as a herd member. Whether you win his heart and become the leader of your "herd of two" will have to do with how and what you communicate.

Are you a brave and resourceful leader?

Are you a low-status herdmate?

Are you just another predator lurking in the bushes?

In reality, you have potential to be all three. Together, we are going to attempt to shift away from the latter and toward the former by paying attention to your horse's behavior and learning to respond to all respectful offers to form a partnership.

There is something else I want to share with you before we start. It concerns one of the reasons I didn't choose a career in horses earlier in my life.

When I was showing horses as a youth competitor, the horse community seemed dominated by feisty and opinionated professionals, who espoused only one way of doing things; it was their way "or the highway." I didn't think I could get along well in such a dogmatic environment; it seemed too oppressive to follow along blindly without the ability to question and innovate.

In recent years, there has been a shift in the way we view horses and our relationship to them in general. We look to the horse to teach us by giving us feedback on how we're doing as partners. In fact, this very honest and precise feedback is what makes horses so valuable as psychotherapy co-facilitators.

What I want to do with this book is to empower you to be a better partner by pointing out and explaining both what is going on with your horse and why it's going on. I don't pretend to have met every quirky horse on earth, but I've been a student long enough to have a working knowledge of horse behavior. That is what I want you to have as a new horse owner.

Occasionally in this book, I've given some examples of horse keeping and horsemanship gone wrong. In many cases, I have tried to present an incident or scenario from my own history. To be sure, I was once new to horse ownership—and have been the owner of a new horse numerous times. I learned much of what I know by realizing what I was doing wasn't working, seeking better answers, and then changing the way I do things. By exposing some of my own blunders and how I overcame them, I'm hoping that it will inspire and encourage you to create a special bond with your new horse.

Finally, in writing this book I have quoted and mentioned the names of some established natural horsemanship clinicians like Pat Parelli, Ray Hunt, and Mark Rashid. There are many other horse professionals who have touched my life and informed my instincts as well, including Dr. Robert Miller (my first vet), Monte Foreman (my first riding teacher), Linda Tellington Jones, Carolyn Resnick, and Ned Leigh. I am in no way proselytizing any particular approach to horsemanship, natural or otherwise. I believe that the horse in front of you will always be the supreme guide to how he thinks and behaves. Just the act of spending time with your horse will begin to educate you regarding not just the species and the breed, but also the unique individual. *Spend the time you need to learn your horse and let him learn you.* You can never go wrong if you always keep that in mind.

Five Signs You May Have a Bonding Issue with Your New Horse

Sign #5 - Butterflies are Free But...

You've had the horse for six months, yet each time you pull up to the stables you get a sense of being in the top chair on the Ferris wheel. Excitement—or anxiety? However you label it, your horse will pick up on that heightened energy. Some horses won't be affected much, but if your horse is reactive enough to become energized around you, take responsibility for the state in which you show up. Instead of proceeding in an anxious or tense condition, spend some time hand walking your animal, curry brush in hand, and letting him graze while you concentrate on breathing, dealing with ANTs (Automatic Negative Thoughts that transmit energy and imagery to other sentient beings) and being in present time. In short, practice mindfulness. In research studies of horse/human interaction, the human's heart rate can lower significantly simply by being with the horse in a non-demanding way. *Bottom line: Let the animal do his magic by re-setting your autonomic nervous system; then proceed on with your plan for a relaxed and fun ride.*

Sign #4 - The Name Game's Gone Lame...

If what you call your horse keeps changing, even after five or six months and several times through the alphabet, not to mention annoying all your friends and ignoring all the name suggestions on your Facebook wall, you need to look at what is keeping that name at bay. It doesn't matter to the horse what you call him, but continually selecting then rejecting a series of stable names over several months suggests that things just aren't settled in someone's mind. *Bottom line: The horse looks to you for leadership and stability. If he doesn't find it, you will lose value in his eyes and he will tune you out.*

Sign #3 - Arrested (Trust) Development...

After six months you are still spending a half hour to 45 minutes "warming up" your horse in the round pen or on a longe line. Really? Did you know that working cowboys and other professional riders mostly don't do that? They catch, saddle, and get on. The "warm-up" happens on the way to the cow pens. If you are simply going down the trail, the warm-up can be the first mile of the ride. Why else would you need to exercise a horse before getting on? Is the chasing and harassing him into a lather in the round pen before saddling up designed to give you a false sense of control? Real control needs closer contact, either on the ground or in the saddle. Control means, for example, asking for just the left hind foot to move forward or backward on cue. Wearing down a horse into obedience is not control and ultimately will only result in a tired yet fearful horse. If your horse has become overly exuberant over the months since you bought him, do a nutrition check. Most pleasure horses can survive just fine on grass hay and vitamins. Poor keepers (those who can't sustain their weight without tons of high calorie feed) should first have teeth and parasite checks performed before you pour on the grain. *Bottom line: Feed high calorie food only after a good relationship has been established and even then only if your riding program is rigorous enough to warrant it.*

Sign #2 - Owner Gone AWOL...

Horses don't text, email, have smart phones, or even a snail mail address; they really can't do Skype! Thus, all the things you use to communicate and make promises to spend more time with your human relationships are lost on your equine buddy. A horse relies on consistent, in-person contact in order to develop a trust bond with a human. If, after six months of ownership, you are still only spending about two to three hours per week with your horse, there is no mystery about why neither of you seem confident in your relationship. Consider taking a day off from work (they're called "mental health" days) and spending it at the stable, just hanging out with your horse. Come early, bringing a book and chair, and just inhabit his space. Take him out of his stall several times, sometimes for structured activity and then some for just grazing and sight seeing. *Bottom line: If you can't pry more time away to bond with your horse, then you may need to examine whether you have enough time to be a horse owner, or whether a leased or rented horse would better serve your needs.*

... And the #1 Sign - That Faraway Look in His Eyes.

If, each time you ask him to perform a task either on the ground or in the saddle, your horse's gaze strays over to his stable mates, the neighbor's green pasture, or the ranch dog walking by, it isn't because he has ADHD—he's just not impressed with your leadership. The next thing that happens is that he forgets he has YOU at his side or on his back. Then chaos arises as he finally wakes up on the trail, thinks he is alone and develops "happy feet" trying to get back to safety. *Bottom line: YOU are his safety and you need to make every attempt to let him know that, as much as possible and as early as possible in your relationship.*

Chapter 1: What Do These Horses Want, Anyway?

"A horse does not care how much you know until he knows how much you care." –Pat Parelli

What is important to a horse? What are his needs? What do these horses want, anyway?

Nearly all college students are exposed to the idea of a hierarchy of needs somewhere in their first semester of Psychology 101. Abraham Maslow developed a theory of human need in the 1940s that explained a persons struggle toward higher awareness and fulfillment. This is illustrated most prominently by Maslow's pyramid, which shows the most basic requirements at the bottom and the most elevated or ethereal needs at the top, i.e. self-esteem and self-actualization.

Self-actualization

Esteem

Social belonging

Shelter, safety, protection

Physiological (health, food, sleep)

Similarly, horses have their own hierarchy of needs that culminate in what I call "herd-happy" behavior. This behavior is most often seen in groups of horses at pasture that start spontaneously running in various directions, often breaking into a series of bucks out of sheer exuberance. It is a *joie de vivre* herd behavior that differs quite a bit from herds that are responding to predator threat. There, the goal is to move efficiently and as one unit in a direction away from danger.

A horse's hierarchy of needs can be viewed as follows:

Herd harmony

Play drive/Dominance

Companionship (herdmates)

Comfort (food, rest, freedom from pain)

Safety/Security (assurance they won't get eaten)

Your horse's most basic need is to be safe from predators. If he feels safe, he'll seek out comfort in the form of food or rest. If his comfort needs are met, he'll seek companionship from his stablemates. If he gets accepted into the herd (more about that later), he'll test out his dominance and play drive on his neighbors. When all needs are met and the herd is in harmony, spontaneous acts of group exuberance will occur.

Most readers of this book will have horses that have already had their needs met up to the companionship level. This means that they are not really in imminent danger of becoming predator food (though they might try and convince you otherwise) and they are not wanting for nourishment, water, or rest. The exception to this would be if you have rescued a horse from an animal rescue or neglectful situation. While it is rewarding to give such a needy horse a better home, these animals often require care that is beyond the knowledge and abilities of a novice horse owner. There is also a great chance that, as the horse improves and moves up the scale of needs, he may not prove to be the best beginners mount. (For my own account of the consequences of such a rescue, read the story of "Bandy" in Chapter Six).

So, where do you fit into the horse's hierarchy of needs? The ideal and short answer is, on every level. From the moment your horse arrives in his new home, you will strive to be the B.O.S.S. of everything that is important to that horse. Now, I don't mean you are going to "show him who's boss" in a fierce battle of muscle and spirit. That belongs to the old paradigm of horse handling. You are simply going to take every opportunity to demonstrate that you are the **Beneficent** and **Omnipotent Source** of **Supply** for all things that are important to him.

In a feral or wild herd, a horse's survival depends on the actions of the leader of that herd, usually a dominant mare. This mare operates instinctively, regulating the herd's survival activities, including when and where to eat, when and where to drink, when to breed and, most crucially, when to get out of the area. Ever vigilant, it is she who raises her head up first at the smallest stirring of trouble. Depending on her nature, she may be actively dominant or a more beneficent leader, guiding by example. Either way, she is the-one-with-the-good-ideas, the Beneficent and Omnipotent Source of Supply, and woe to any lower status herd member that doesn't heed her communications!

A Good B.O.S.S. Creates a Herd Happy Environment

While there may not be the same threat to the herd in domestic situations, horses are left with the instinct to seek out and follow the-one-with-the-good-ideas, or the B.O.S.S. Creating situations that demonstrate to your horse that you are the person for the job takes some ingenuity and creativity. Still, the result will be a horse that trusts your judgment—one that believes in your leadership, no matter what the environment may be telling him.

Ironically, in our endeavor to make domestic horses more useful, we often make horse keeping choices that further distance the animals from their needs. Wild horses are survivors, having adapted to the various terrains and climates in which they live. Except for the quantity that are captured by the Bureau of Land Management and destined to live in pens until they are auctioned off, wild horse herds roam freely 24 hours a day, seven days a week, in all four seasons. They don't graze on lush pastures, but instead browse through acres and acres of inedible or undesirable vegetation in search of sustenance. They are constantly on the move, traveling over rocks and other terrain harsh enough to grind their hooves down to sharp, flinty nubs. Rarely do they visit the same blade of grass or even patch of ground that was grazed in prior weeks or months. This means they have a slim chance of parasite infestation and virtually no need for chemical deworming. However, should they feel the need to purge internal invaders, there are indigenous plants they can actively seek out for that purpose.

In the wild, herd harmony is often maintained with a rigorous vigil by the lead mare. This results in little need for artificial barriers between feuding animals. A rude or misbehaving horse, often a young male, is ostracized from the group until he learns some manners (or manages to steal a mare or two and set up his own herd). The remaining horses enjoy the easy companionship that communal living affords. *There is no such thing as social phobia or mental illness in a wild horse heard.*

We have moved our domestic horses away from this model. We erect barns to house our animals and in doing so often seal out fresh air and seal in the toxic fumes created by their excrement. In those barns, we isolate our horses, sometimes not even allowing them to see each other. Living in cramped quarters means the horses learn to litter where they eat, thus ensuring they will re-infest their system with the same parasites they expel. It also sets them up for contracting thrush, a chronic fungal disorder of the hoof.

Lacking pasture or acreage for our horses to graze on, and desiring a horse that is "in good flesh"—meaning, plump and shiny—we feed cultivated legume hay that can be overly rich in calories, carbohydrates, and protein. We supplement with carbohydrate-rich grain products that have been sweetened and laced with vitamins. While feeding vitamins is a good idea, particularly for young and growing horses, the extra calories supplied by the starch and sugars can create metabolic and behavioral problems in many horses. Diseases of the hoof, such as laminitis and founder, are also commonly related to an overly rich diet.

In the interest of keeping our horse's coat sleek and manageable, we start keeping a blanket or sheet on him at night, and sometimes even during the day. Once winter has arrived and he's grown used to the extra protection, we must continue the ritual of covering him daily, thereby diminishing his ability to keep himself warm. Because he spends his days on soft sand or shavings instead of natural terrain, the feet of the domestic horse aren't worn down properly and start to lose their shape as they grow out.

All this explains why we need the regular intervention of various specialists like farriers and veterinarians in order to keep our horses healthy and functioning, while their feral counterparts need none of them.

When I first started keeping my own horses as an adult, I committed many of the horse keeping faux pas I've just described. I fed alfalfa hay, which was cheap and plentiful, stuffing it into a feeder that hung on a wall, high above ground level. I put shoes on my horses because that's how I was used to handling hoof issues. I stabled my horses separately, blanketed them daily, and used a dewormer six times a year, all out of habit. (Did I mention that all these practices add up to a lot of manual labor, not to mention extra expense?

In the last two decades, I've had a chance to assess and revise my horse keeping; I've modified practices to better address my horses' needs and preferences as well as my desire to labor less. For instance:

- Their turnout is almost exclusively the decomposed granite that exists in their high desert environment. I have built some rocky sections on which the horses can wear their feet down.
- I feed grass hay, supplementing calories for the two older horses in the form of a pelleted product designed for seniors. I spread the grass over a large area, including on hillsides in order to approximate the browsing they so enjoy.
- Before using a dewormer, I get their manure analyzed by a veterinary lab to determine the existence of a parasite infestation. There is no point in spending the money and adding chemicals to my horses' system unless it's absolutely necessary.

Like many individual horse keepers, I don't have large acreage set aside for my horses. In fact, the entire horse operation covers only half of our five-plus acre property. This isn't a lot of space for a browsing animal. Truthfully, I would need a pasture that was at least four to five acres for each horse in order to sustain them 24/7. So, in my "modified plan" I let my horses out of their pens to meander around the stable area for about 10 to 14 hours a day. This not only allows the horses to graze on the hay I've spread around in many small piles, it also satisfies their need to associate freely. I watch them pair up or walk around from group to group and it seems that they are better able to manifest their own temperament and status. In choosing who they want to hang out with, they are less apt to pick the kinds of fights that lead to vet bills. In short, they are beginning to display signs of "herd harmony."

This freedom also seems to make them more sociable with people. It's not uncommon for one or more of the herd to greet my guests and me as we come through the stable yard gate. Even Travis, a socially phobic retired show horse, has taken to wandering up to take a gander at the array of human clients and students who come through the gate.

Periodically in this book, I'll mention more ways in which you can increase your horse's awareness of you as the B.O.S.S. in his environment. For instance, the very simple act of grooming is a great way to establish yourself as a valuable source of both comfort and companionship. We normally think of grooming as a human construct, i.e., something done with specific brushes, combs and rags that tidies up a horse and makes him presentable for competition or exhibition. However the idea of grooming was born out of feral herd behavior, where horses stand and nibble or massage each other's withers and backs, often for hours. Walking around a pasture of horses, you might see mutual nibbling as well as single horses rubbing on trees, or rolling in bare, sandy areas. All of these qualify as "natural" grooming behaviors, which release a steady supply of endorphins into the horses' biochemistry.

This may account for why most horses willingly stand still to be groomed. In fact, the only horse I ever met that didn't like to be groomed had some back issues. The nerves in his spine and hip area were so aggravated that the slightest touch on his side would elicit a defensive response from him; it was not unlike the human condition of fibromyalgia. Eventually, the gelding was helped through some sessions of equine therapy work, including acupressure, acupuncture and chiropractic. Today, when I go to visit him, his back problems have long since subsided and he sidles up to me for some grooming, the same as any other horse.

First Bonding

What a delight it is for a foal to discover that humans come with flexible groomers at the ends of their arms! When they get their first taste of "scritching," you'll see the little noses stuck in the air with pleasure, the top lip quivering in rhythm to your scratching fingers. This discovery that humans can provide something of value, which far exceeds what an equine can offer, is often the first step toward bonding.

With the two Premarin fillies I adopted, the art of grooming became not just a game but also the single means of communicating with them initially. After some rude handling and an abrupt departure from her mother in Saskatchewan, Canada, not to mention the brutally long trailer ride to Arizona, Twinkle—the first of my fillies—came to me as a hostile and suspicious six-month-old. I would sit inside her manger as she alternately approached to nibble some hay and retreated to stand eyeing me with a look of profound distrust.

After weeks of talking and even singing to her, one day she let me put a hand on her neck for just an instant. The next day, it was a few instants, and the next, I able to gently rub on her shoulder before she stepped off to stand haughtily in the corner. Eventually, I was gently scrubbing her neck and shoulder area with my fingernails, paying attention to where she responded most. This one action of providing comfort and companionship began to unlock the sweetness and innocence that was hiding just beneath all that hostile suspicion. It is a terrible thing to witness a weanling who has already developed such a strong negative opinion about people. Quite honestly it still informs some of her behavior today, almost a decade later. However, learning how baby Twinkle liked to be groomed became the first step toward winning her trust in me as her B.O.S.S.

Like all good things, there is a dark side of grooming that must be addressed. Some horses will become so comfortable with humans grooming them that they turn it into a domination game.

In the herd, the horse whose idea it is to be groomed is usually the more dominant. She will approach a beta, or less dominant horse, and say "Okay, you're it. Let's groom." The same dominant horse may deflect an approach by a beta horse with sounds and body language that say, "How dare you presume!" Thus, if you are with your horse at liberty and he approaches you and insists on grooming by stepping into your space and bumping you with his head or shoulder, you might consider whether that horse is being respectful of your status in your "herd of two." In such cases, I usually ask the horse to swing their back end away from me, disengaging their hindquarters, or step backward from pressure applied to the chest or nose. Then I reward their response with the desired grooming. This establishes what a B.O.S.S. should always strive to possess—an attitude that is kind but firm.

On Naming Your Horse

Horses don't really care what you call them, as long as you refer to them consistently. This is part of my own addendum to their hierarchy of needs—the need for a horse's human to develop a consistent way of handling him. A name is the first step in creating that consistency. This is true even with a horse that seems to thrive on variety in his activities, requiring you to be very creative in your arena work to combat boredom. You still need to commit to a name for that horse before you will truly start to bond. Nothing communicates better to a horse that "Hey, you're not going to be here for very long" or "Hey, you're not any more special to me than this dirt clod" like not deciding on a name.

I recently shamed some good friends of mine into finally selecting names for their trail horses—a lovely matched pair of bays. I did this in a very sneaky way. They dropped them off at my place for boarding and went off on a 10-day trip. Before they left, I asked for the horses' names. Tom—a cowboy in his sixties—said, "Well, we don't really have set names for them." I was taken aback, as they'd had those horses for years. While they were gone, I promptly gave the horses—a mare and gelding—the names "Tristan" and "Isolde," and told Tom so when he came to fetch them. He screwed up his face like he'd bitten into a lemon, but said nothing about my audacity. The next time we rode together, Tom made a point of referring to the horses by their new names, "Luke" and "Stella."

Some people think that changing a horse's name is bad luck, or at least bad form. I want to assure you that lightening will not strike you down if you decide to change your new horse's name. How you refer to a horse is important in both how the name sounds and what it signifies...both to you *and* the horse, strange as that seems.

Of the horses that came to me with names, I've probably changed more of them than I have kept the original. I like to give a name that is a positive message to the horse and meaningful to me. For instance, the gelding I refer to as "Goodman" in this book came to me with the registered name "Badger's Commission," shortened to just "Badger." I got a sense from his owner that he was already a handful. (Maybe it was the hand-scrawled message "This horse is crazy!" across his vet records.) So, I thought about having to say the word "bad" every time I summoned the gelding or referred to him in conversation and knew that name would have to go. Then it was as simple as saying, "I want a name that sounds positive like... good... good boy...good... Goodman." The name fit him (the runner-up was my five-year-old son's choice of "Mr. Ed") and it became his stable name for the next 20 years.

I also renamed my mare Nikki when she arrived at my stable. Her previous owner had gotten her at Mingus Mountain Academy—a residential facility for girls with behavioral problems. The man had been out in the paddock looking at the school's young stock and a playful young Andalusian-cross mare had snuck up behind him and taken the wallet out of his back pocket. Since her registered name was "My Scooter"—and even he knew that was a ridiculous name for a beautiful Spanish-bred mare—he named her "Pickpocket." Ye-es that's right—Pickpocket. I'm sure it reminded him of the way they'd "met cute" at the home for wayward girls.

Since I don't go in much for names with more than two syllables, I went searching for a nice and easy moniker that would retain some of the same sounds—for the sake of consistency. The mare looked sort of Mediterranean to me—pale body and jet-black mane and tail—so I happened upon a name I could envision an Italian pronouncing with a lilt in his voice, "Oh-ah Nee-kee, don-ta tawk like dat."

My favorite name story happened just recently and shows the power that making a name change can have. Over the past few years I've increased my therapy herd to include two Falabella miniature horses. The Falabella strain was developed in Argentina by a family of the same name. For some reason, the diminutive breed (my two stand 26 and 28 inches) is referred to as a horse and not a pony. In recent times the Fallabella has found its way to the U.S. as a trendy novelty pet.

"Elvis" was the first to arrive at my place—a small grey and black spotted gelding with the stubby legs and lush mane and tail that are typical of Falabellas. I was told that he was a reject from a local horse therapy program and had also been in and out of several other homes. His current owners were desperate to place him.

"He's just so full of energy and, well, high jinks—not a good match with a child, I'm afraid," the woman explained. She lifted up the hair that hid a large bulge on his forehead. "See? That's why they call him Elvis. He's got a pomp-a-dour!" (Actually, we now like to refer to it as the "brain bump" where he stores his huge intellect.)

Once he was at my ranch, I soon saw what got the mini booted out of a children's therapy program. Not a real respecter of personal space, he liked to try and crawl up the sides of people who had the misfortune to choose him for equine activities. He tried to ram into my lead mare, Nikki, who soon sent him flying. He got "fresh" with another mare, Twinkle, and she chased him around the pasture for a half hour. After he tried unsuccessfully to steal dinner from my towering draft-cross, Paloma, I sequestered him in a run at the far end of the stable and despaired of ever integrating him into the herd without him becoming a furry pancake.

That was when we got a second mini gelding to be Elvis' buddy. Whimsically, I named the new mini "Arlo," in homage to another musical talent, Arlo Guthrie. And so began the rockin' duo of Elvis and Arlo.

A year or so later, I had taken on the mentorship of a high school student named Alec. At just 16, he was deeply interested in pursuing equine-assisted work, as it relates to experiential education and psychotherapy. I asked Alec—a strapping young man with a blond buzz cut—to exercise the miniature horses and my lesson horse Travis on a weekly basis. He was also to interact with them in many of the ways that my students and clients would. In essence, he would be helping the three newest horses hone their therapeutic skills.

One day, Alec sauntered up after he'd done a round pen session with the minis and casually leaned on the fence, scratching his close-cropped head.

"What was Arlo's name before he came here?" he queried tentatively.

"Um, what? Oh, let's see...Thunder?...Lightning? Lightning, I think. Horrible name," I answered, distracted with tacking up another horse. "So...trite... just because he's white, I guess."

Alec cleared his throat. "Actually... he prefers that name."

"...he *prefers* Lightning?" I asked, keeping my voice level and trying not to smirk.

"To the one you gave him. He doesn't understand it when you call him that."

"Oh." I was caught off-guard by Alec's earnestness. He was obviously committed to what he was saying.

"Well then..." I said, feeling like a heel. "By all means... call him... um, Lightning then. See if that helps."

Not much had been known of the little gelding's previous situation, but he seemed to carry a profound air of sadness with him everywhere. He was very protective of his body when being handled and his response to anyone approaching him in his pen was to run away and hide. When he'd arrived, I'd noticed his tail was ragged and short, ending just below the dock. The texture of the hair was coarse, frizzy and discolored orange...exactly what burnt hair or fur looks like. Since we don't have much of his story prior to arriving, other than he belonged to a middle-school aged girl, I can only imagine what had caused such a condition.

Though reticent with humans, the white mini had no problem establishing himself in the horse herd. He counteracted Elvis' aggressive first greeting with high screams and flailing hooves and soon got the upper hand in their relationship. Though Elvis quite possibly deserved them, the white mini's angry explosions were painful to watch nonetheless. I had thought I was giving him a new start by renaming him, but maybe I'd gotten that wrong.

Some months later, I observed Alec working with the-mini-now-known-as-Lightning in the round pen. The gelding did look more energetic and confident; he seemed to carry himself a bit better. I decided it was a good call by Alec and went to do other chores. Before long, Alec was at my side again.

"You know, Elvis doesn't really like his name, either."

"Well, I didn't give Elvis his name," I retorted. "He came lamely named—or...well...that's how he arrived...pre-named." By now, I was feeling a bit defensive about the whole naming issue.

"The name's too..."—Alec gestured wide with his hands—"big for him. A big rock star with a reputation for excess, right? I think it's part of what makes him misbehave."

"Oh, so that's what's doing it," I quipped, trying to humor my protégé. "Well, I'll take it under advisement."

During that week, I happened to be grooming the little spotted horse one day and something dawned on me as I ran the brush down his feathery legs and over his grotesquely dished and spotted face. At only twenty-six inches tall, he looked like a horse that had stepped right out of a J.R.R. Tolkien book. He looked just like a hobbit's mount! For a moment, I was lost in the vision of Frodo or some other Lord of the Rings character leaping on the back of this miniscule charger and racing off to capture the precious golden ring—the first of many adventures they would have...

"Elf," I said to him, "that's what you are. You're a little elfin creature." And that is how "Elvis the Puffed Up Rock Star" became "Elf the mini." Elf has shown himself to be much better behaved than Elvis could have ever imagined. Elf is respectful with his peers and has turned into a gem of a therapy horse. He stands at a child's side for lengths of time without ever feeling the need to sink his teeth into something. Elvis was fractious on the ground and dangerous to drive (another reason he was ejected from several homes) but as I sat on a stool and groomed his long fluffy mane, the mini-now-known-as-Elf leaned his side against me and sighed with contentment. Now with a label that fit, it seemed like the little horse wanted nothing more than to preserve the harmony of the moment. Indeed, there is no finer Elf in all the kingdom...

Five Things to Do Right Now to Help Form a Closer Bond with Your Horse

1. **Reward your horse's efforts to get into a learning state of mind.** Whenever you see your horse licking and chewing, stop and reward his efforts to reduce his own stress and tension. A horse that is encouraged to relax will be more receptive to forming an alliance with a human.

2. **Resolve never let your horse approach you with his ears pinned back.** Some horses seem to do this "unconsciously," but it is still an attempt at dominating behavior. Keep sending the horse away, politely and without emotion, until his ears prick forward and stay that way as he approaches. Hint: If he seems less than interested in approaching in the first place, bring an empty feed bucket with you. Works like a charm.

3. **Learn to ignore the wrong response in addition to rewarding the proper one.** Again, don't put any emotion or attitude into the way you ignore the wrong response. Simply ask again for him to do something and wait for the proper response before releasing pressure and rewarding.

4. **Spend at least one hour desensitizing your horse to one of his "horse monsters."** This can be plastic bags, a tarp, the hose, etc. Even if his response isn't completely "flat" by the end of the hour, reward all licking and chewing behavior, and know that it is still better than it was. (See Item #1).

5. **Learn some stretching exercises you can do to help relax and release your horse's muscles before and after riding.** Equine masseuses will tell you that when they arrive at the barn for body work sessions, some of their regular clients call out to them like long lost lovers!

Chapter 2: Horses Draw Lines in the Sand

"If your horse says no, you either asked the wrong question, or asked the question wrong." —Pat Parelli

"You know horses are smarter than people. You never heard of a horse going broke betting on people." —Will Rogers

As has been mentioned previously, horses don't like change. Change in their environment could signal a dangerous situation, and one that threatens their survival. Change requires them to go on alert, scour the area for predators, and make snap judgments regarding whether the neighbor's brand new mailbox has teeth or if the tree branch that fell overnight is actually harboring a cougar.

If you are taking your new horse on that scenic mountain trail for the first time, be prepared to step across many "lines in the sand" or thresholds, especially if you go out solo. If you pay attention, you can learn to spot the warning signs that a threshold is approaching. The horse will:

- Raise his head higher
- Stare without blinking
- Prick his ears forward (the ears will be tense and hard to bend)
- Quicken his breathing and/or snort audibly
- Begin to take smaller, quicker steps ~or~
- Slow down and come to a complete stop while staring fixedly at something of concern.

The horse that has come to a stop is saying, in essence, "This far and no farther until I'm reassured that what I'm looking at is not on the list of known predators." While some riders may be able to convince their horses to move ahead through coercion, a better solution is to allow the horse to stand where he is, gather enough information to satisfy himself that the object or situation is safe for passage, and keep your leg and rein contact steady and firm. By doing this, you are saying back to him, "I know you have a trust problem right now, my friend, and I am here to support you in facing down this menace."

While others may disagree, I've found the best solution for some stalled out and spooked horses is to dismount and lead them right up to the object—provided it isn't a cougar after all. The idea is to stand up to, or even "chase" away, the threat, thus demonstrating to your horse that you are a worthy leader and protector of the herd.

I employed such a tactic a few years ago when I hauled two young mares I was training to a ranch in California for the summer. We had no sooner unloaded in the stable area than some extremely nosy Nubian goats ran up to greet the new arrivals. The mares took one look at the fast approaching goats— the likes of which they'd never seen before—and proceeded to try and reload themselves in the trailer. Instinctively, I turned and ran at the goats, chasing them back down the road and tugging on the mares' lead ropes so they had to follow me. It wasn't long before the mares were running alongside me, emboldened by the fun game of "Chase the Goat." From that point on, neither of the horses blinked an eye at the pet goats, who freely roamed the stables all summer.

By chasing away an intruder to our herd of three, I had elevated myself to the role of leader. This "protecting the herd" is an exercise I use in my coaching for horse and rider pairs. Basically, I have a student bring their horse into an arena where one or two horses are loose. Being social animals, loose horses will usually come to inspect any horse that enters their space, especially if they suspect it is a lower status horse that needs some "schooling" on social etiquette.

The student's task is to wait until the approaching horse is five or ten feet away, then drive the intruder off with the end of a lead rope. In this way, the human protects his "herd of two" and begins to build the horse's trust in his leadership. After a while, this trust building will allow the horse to overcome his skepticism about his new environment and begin to bond with his new herd leader...his human.

Not every horse is fearful of new environments, though. Some veterans of the competitive world have "been there, done that," having spent countless hours on the road traveling from venue to venue. In such cases, they may be quite desensitized to the sights and sounds that might make a less seasoned horse quake, i.e.:

- Loudspeakers bleating announcements and music
- Flags and banners
- Crowds of people
- Large diesel trucks honking their horns
- Buses and other traffic zooming by on the Interstate.

Yet, take these same horses up a mountain trail and they might not be able to tolerate strange rock formations and the unadulterated smell of wild predators.

My lesson horse Travis is an example of such a veteran. He was just turning 15 when he joined my herd of therapy horses, having spent most of his adult life carrying youngsters around the show ring. I marveled at how calm and professional he was when we hauled to weeklong clinics, where he performed with the same poise as if we were back in my arena.

The first time he and I ventured out on the trail, just a few weeks after I'd hauled him from his smooth-hilled, coastal California to the wilds of the Arizona high desert, an entirely different story unfolded. It was an early March afternoon when I saddled him up and headed out solo on just a trail ride of an hour and a half. One of my staunchest beliefs is that you build trust by taking slow, short, even boring rides with a new or nervous animal. That way, you prove to them repeatedly that nothing scary or unpleasant happens on the trail—you don't get hurt and you don't get eaten.

I forgot all that when I ran into my neighbor Alison and her daughter Caroline on the same trail. We decided to do a longer loop and take advantage of the unseasonably warm winter day. This is where my seasoned trooper of a kid's horse began to slowly lose his mind.

When I'd first started riding Travis, I noticed he was quite defensive around other horses. He preferred to spend time off by himself rather than venture into potentially dangerous herd dynamics. Would he survive in the wild with such an attitude? Probably not. Allegiance to and acceptance in a herd is one of the primary survival tools for a feral horse. (On the positive side, Travis has absolutely no issues with "barn sourness"—which is usually the reason horses make it back home from rides in double the time it took to ride out.)

His previous owner had said something vague about a fire evacuation where he'd been thrown in with a lot of aggressive horses and had been banged up pretty badly. Apparently his experience still haunted him the day I rode him out and could account for his sudden drop in confidence when we met up with the other riders.

Sure enough, as the horses drew near, his head came up, his ears pricked, his feet grew quite light and he began to jog as if in a parade, except that we were picking our way through mesquite and scrub oak on the side of a hill. Exacerbating the situation was Travis' first introduction to cat's claw on that very same ride. For the uninitiated, cat's claw (*Acacia greggii*) is a brutal Arizona plant that hooks into passersby and attempts to rip pieces of flesh (or fur) off their bodies. In Travis' case, the first time he forged through a thicket of cat's claw I'm pretty sure he was ready to trade all his exciting adventures in Arizona for a return to his bland, boring, pricker-free life in California.

Suffice it to say that by the end of our ride, Travis and I were more at odds than we had been in our whole three weeks together. I had tried to reassure him throughout, but clearly his thought was, "I'm scratched (in pain), I'm nervous (feeling insecure and unsafe) and these horses simply will not do as companions. You are definitely NOT my herd leader!" Dealing with Travis' unique needs has helped me to realize that not every horse reacts the same to "textbook stimuli." Sometimes you need to tune in and think outside the box.

What ended up working for Travis was to remove him from any threats, including having stable mates near enough to try and steal his food or give him the "stink eye." I put him in a pen on the far side of the horse barn where he could see the other horses but could also feel secure that his "stuff" wouldn't be messed with. Then, I began to provide the quiet, undemanding companionship that would make him feel secure and comfortable. We walked... he grazed... I groomed his back with my fingers... Other horses came near and I drove them off like any good lead mare would. After months of practicing this, one day he chose to leave his food to walk with me as I moved around his turnout, picking up manure. Sometimes it's the little moments that build the bond.

The Intros and Extras of Horse Behavior

Just as there are introverted and extraverted humans, there are distinctive behaviors in the equine population that lean toward indwelling and outgoing personalities. These different polarizations—outward and inward—will tend to make two horses behave differently under the same circumstances. For example, an extraverted horse with a lot of dominance or play drive might "draw a line in the sand" and use aggression or physical intimidation to keep you from crossing it. An example of this is a horse that blocks your access to his left side with his head and shoulders, and sometimes his teeth, when he sees you approaching with the saddle.

Conversely an introvert may simply pull back and try to distance himself from you and the saddle. An introverted horse with a strong domination drive might draw a line halfway up the horse trailer ramp. You can get him up to a certain point, and then dynamite wouldn't make him move any farther into the trailer. Put pressure on an extravert and he may try to escalate the game, moving his feet so much (i.e. rearing, bucking, charging) that he intimidates you into backing down. Still, all of these are signs that your horse doesn't trust you to keep him safe and comfortable in a particular situation. Overcoming that resistance often requires concentrating on other tasks that don't generate as strong a response, then building on the small successes that lead up to the bigger task.

For example, horses are famously claustrophobic, wreaking havoc on most of our plans that involve shoehorning them into a horse trailer—in a hurry—on the morning of some event. While it is optimum to practice trailer loading when there are no time concerns and resulting anxiety about being late for some check-in or registration, our tendency is not to have done the "homework" and to just try and trick or intimidate the horse into cooperating on the spot.

You greet the horse at his stall and he reads the stress in your body, smells it on your breath, and hears it in the tremor of your voice. Line drawn. Not getting a favorable read on the whole situation. Definitely not getting in that tin can trap of a trailer. Hours later, emotions haven't receded and now the horse is as upset as you are. The extravert is dangerously impulsive, "walking tall" and throwing his weight around; the introvert is frozen in place on the ramp, jaw set and plotting how to sabotage any of your plans to ride him in the near future. You decide to trash your agenda for the day and end up parking your trailer. Score one for the horse and zero for building a stronger bond of trust. In short, loading in a trailer can make or break your relationship with your new horse.

The way to approach trailer loading is to make the trailer a familiar item in the horse's environment, as early as possible. I have always put a trailer in with my younger horses so that they can inspect it thoroughly, eat their meals out of it, and congregate inside at free will.

In fact one of my mares, Paloma, the second to arrive as a Premarin foal at the age of six months, refused to be handled or even haltered for almost eight weeks after I got her home. She was clearly traumatized by her previous experiences with humans on the PMU farm and her subsequent 2500-mile trip from Canada to Arizona. Since she seemed to feel safest staying in my trailer, I simply erected a small fenced area around it and there she stayed, freely hopping in and out of the trailer as she liked. To this day, she is the easiest trailer loader on my place.

This free-choice trailer loading will often remove much of the "phobia" from the normally claustrophobic horse. Once the horse is familiar with the look, smell, and feel of the trailer, I make a game of approaching and retreating from the open end of the trailer. I may ask him to load into and out of the trailer dozens of times—for a whole day, if necessary, until he's practically begging to do something more exciting.

What I want to emphasize is not a set way of teaching a horse to load, but a relaxed approach that allows a horse to say "no" a hundred times before he feels trusting enough to crawl into a tight space and allow you to shut the door on him. While I'll never end on an overt "no" from my horse, I will end a loading session on a forward try from him—a definite "maybe."

The Danger of Missing Subtle Cues

Sometimes the clues to a horse's threshold are very subtle—an ear flick, a staring eye, a held breath. The rider or handler may not recognize that the horse has just become unconfident. This can be very dangerous, as the next thing a horse does is often impulsive.

A horse doesn't have to be new to catch you off-guard with a subtle threshold. I had just returned from spending a week at a natural horsemanship clinic with my then three-year-old filly Twinkle. Excited to continue working on natural horsemanship with her, I took her for a casual trail ride the morning after we returned.

It had been a grueling 11-hour trip back from Colorado and we were all pretty exhausted. When the neighbor's dog emerged to snap at the filly's heels, I failed to notice when she began to carry her head higher and had stopped blinking, two signs that she had lost her confidence. The next thing that happened undid her entirely, although it was quite a simple thing. She rooted her head down and grabbed a small tree branch in her mouth. It rattled against her face and the quiet little mare that never hurried anywhere and that liked to stubbornly set her hip against my lateral leg cues suddenly executed a series of very precise and warp speed spins to get away from the menacing branch.

Around, and around, and around we went. After three years of thinking I knew every aspect of this horse's behavior, I was so surprised by the sudden impulsion that I lost my seat and dove off hands first. Later on in the E.R., while waiting for an x-ray of my broken wrist, I would reflect on the business with the dog, which was the "thing that happened before the thing that happened, happened," as natural horsemanship clinician Pat Parelli would say.

While we can't always catch all of the warning behaviors that a horse is going "right-brain," i.e., to the intractable, fearful, and hyper-reactive side of the brain, studying general horse behavior and psychology can help build our awareness regarding what is going on with a horse before his actions escalate into a full blow-up.

A Trial By Fire

One of the reasons we need to master leadership over horses is that some day it might make the difference in an emergency. Such was the case during my summer in California in 2006. My sister Kiki owns and operates the ranch where I grew up and our family raised horses. Occasionally, Kiki and I do sister favors for each other, which is how I found myself traveling with my two mares to take care of her ranch for the summer, the same summer those mares learned to push Kiki's goats around.

A singer-songwriter and musician by trade, Kiki has toured the world with such artists as Chicago, Al Jarreau, Tracie Chapman, and Christopher Cross. This has proven to be a dilemma for her on more than one occasion, as she also runs a 35-acre horse boarding facility that needs daily management. Always up for a new adventure, I looked at the pending summer duties as a chance to pursue both my riding and writing projects. However, the ranch work was about to prove far more demanding—and exciting—than I had anticipated.

The first few weeks just flew by as I oversaw the ranch operations and barely had time to do much riding—let alone writing! When Kiki's husband, Steve came home unexpectedly from his own tour management job halfway through the summer, I moved out onto the house's screened porch to give him some privacy and continued on with my ranch duties. From where I slept on the porch of the 90-year-old adobe ranch house, the stable was partially visible, shrouded by a large grove of oak trees down in the valley the ranch shares with its neighbor, Malibu Creek State Park.

One night, I was just about to tuck myself in when I noticed a glow through the trees in the location of the stables. My first thought was, "Ahhhh great, did I leave the work lights on in the barn again? Then I saw that the glow wasn't steady, it was flickering. I felt adrenaline begin to flush through my body as realization set in. Fire, I thought. Fire at the stables!

I opened the door and shouted into the house that there was a fire at the barn. Steve barely replied, but in what seemed like an instant he was on the porch dressed in a full fireman's suit. I was more than taken aback, then remembered that Steve was actually trying to get work as a fireman; he'd recently completed his training at the fire academy and even had his own fire engine parked down near the stables. He told me to dial 911 and took off to get his truck.

After making the call, I got dressed and made a mental inventory of the horses. Counting my two, there were about fifteen horses to be secured and accounted for. I needed to call their owners and most importantly, I needed to relocate the horses that were stabled in the barn that stood adjacent to the blaze.

Half of the ranch's stable sits across a small deep creek, which bisects it from the paddocks and arena. The means of crossing the creek is a bridge that once had been a flatbed railroad car. Leading or riding a horse over the bridge creates a metallic, rasping sound that had greatly unnerved my two young mares the first dozen times their hooves came in contact with it. Luckily, they were in a paddock on the safe side of the creek, but there were at least five other horses that needed evacuation.

The closer I got to the stable, the better view of the blaze I had. There was a line of fire not 50 feet from the back of the barn, slowly devouring dried vegetation as it crept closer. Meanwhile, I could hear sirens in the distance and figured it wouldn't be long before the professionals arrived. This was the time to get the horses across the bridge.

After sequestering the seven ranch dogs in the house, I ran down the hill to the stable. At the end stall, I felt around for the halter and lead rope I knew would be hanging there. In the dark, Sofia, a tall and sleek Quarter Horse show filly pushed her nose into my hands. I'd handled her some as she belonged to my sister Cathy, and knew she would be one of the easy ones. I haltered her and led her down the aisle past a pair of snorting endurance Arabians and Kiki's personal mounts, Rose and August.

As we started across the metal bridge in semidarkness, I caught sight of movement at my feet. I looked down and saw a fire hose snaking across the bridge; somewhere beyond the stable, an unseen Steve was yanking it closer to the fire. Sofia was taking a good look at it too, but blessedly she kept moving with me. We got over to firm ground and I trotted her over to the first paddock. All of the paddocks on this side had been designated to single boarded horses, so I'd decided to put all my family members' horses together to make room for the evacuees. In went Sofia with my Twinkle and Paloma.

I held my breath as I ran back to get the next horse. She was a petite grey Arab with a great many endurance miles on her. She also turned out to be surprisingly calm, considering I'd never really handled her, the stench of smoke was everywhere, the hose was still slithering along the bridge, and now the first of the fire trucks had arrived with strobing red lights. In she went to the first empty paddock, and back I went for the third horse.

This one, a leggy Arab gelding, was a bigger challenge. Having been "the one left behind" by his stable mate, he nearly yanked me off my feet in his haste to join her on the other side of the creek. That was until he saw the writhing hose. He stopped in his tracks at the beginning of the bridge and gaped at the heavy white canvas hose that two firemen were now yanking and looping to hasten its journey. I got between horse and hose and did the first thing that came to mind. I covered his closest eye with my left hand and jerked his lead rope forward with my right. He bellowed for his stable mate, who returned his call. Then he half-dragged me off my feet as I tried to run sideways across the bridge, up a small hill and to the paddock where the grey was waiting. Three down, two to go.

Rose and August were pacing in their adjacent pens. They were the counterparts to my mares, Twinkle and Paloma i.e., Premarin "byproduct" foals that had been adopted via the Internet. Kiki had put years of work into their training, but right now I was counting on their good natures, and their familiarity with me, their "auntie." Once haltered, I led August first and had Rose follow him. I figured that would work, as lead mares like Rose don't consider it following so much as driving from behind. They would have to go single file over the bridge in order to avoid the hose and any fire personnel.

And there were personnel and equipment everywhere. I could see trucks parked in every inch of space in the parking area beyond the bridge. The shouting and the noise of a dozen diesel engines reached an almost surreal din. As we came to the bridge, about twenty men with axes and shovels were making their way across. I heard them say the wind had changed and the fire was climbing up the hill. There was no way to get to it except by foot and helicopter drops.

Rose was pushing on August's rump to hurry him along. August began to get agitated and bumped into me, knocking me off balance and almost off the bridge. I shook the mare's rope to back her off his rump a bit, a handy Parelli technique called the "Yo-Yo Game," which I never would have imagined I'd be using on a night like this. It worked long enough for us to get across the bridge. Then the three of us ran shoulder to shoulder to the last paddock where we were greeted by four eager new friends.

Most of the rest of that night, I sat on a hill with the seven ranch dogs and watched the men work on the fire. In the paddocks below, the horses did the same thing. All petty disputes and any herd dominance were put on hold as they stood mesmerized by the flames and activity.

The fire had evoked the memory of another time at that same ranch when I was fourteen. Along with my two siblings, I was given the responsibility of moving our seven horses to safety. That time, a vast brush fire had been approaching from the far northwest side of the San Fernando Valley, whipped by the savage Santa Ana winds off the Mohave Desert. It was raging along the sole access road to the ranch. A giant plume of red and grey smoke towered over our property, blotting out the sun. Our escape plan was to saddle up the ranch horses and ride south, toward the Pacific Ocean, leading our prized show horses. My sisters and I finally made it to Mulholland Drive, where emergency volunteers loaded up our horses and hauled them to safety.

The thing I've learned about being in the midst of such an evacuation is that it clarifies your choices and timeline. You don't stop and question your abilities as a horsewoman. You assume leadership and take action to bring your beloved animals—or someone else's—to safety.

Five Top Tips for Emergencies That New Horse Owners May Overlook

#1 – Keep your horse trailer in good condition and truck tanked up. If you rely on others for transport, keep a list of at least three reliable haulers you can call in an emergency.

#2 – Have current photos of all your animals in case of evacuation. In addition, make up an ID tag for your horse's halter with your name and contact info on it.

#3 – If your horse is not good at trailer loading, especially under pressured conditions, consult with your veterinarian on sedation options, but BE SURE you or someone on site can confidently perform any necessary procedures. Remember that an overmedicated horse can be just as dangerous as a non-medicated one.

#4 – Have a plan in place if you aren't able to evacuate your horse. Ideally, locate a cleared fenced area on high ground that would be safe from fire, flood, and mayhem.

#5 – Check into your community's disaster preparedness procedures. Some rural and equestrian communities have citizen volunteer teams that assist the fire and police professionals with animal management and relocation during disasters. Join one if you can!

Chapter 3: You Don't Have to Be Bossy to Be the B.O.S.S

"Make the wrong thing hard and the right thing easy."—Ray Hunt

"There are many ways to do something, but not many ways to do something right."—Bruce Jackson

When I was about ten, I got my first horse—a Mustang I named Bonfire—which my family proceeded to nickname "Bon-Bon" despite my vehement protests.

The fact that I couldn't dissuade them from the silly, repetitive name may speak volumes about my people skills at that age. We had just moved to a new community, which meant leaving my birthplace with its familiar neighborhood haunts and school chums behind. My abilities to bond and make new friends were being tested and I was finding them to be sorely lacking. I was about to enter into a very lonely and isolated pre-adolescence, which is how an emaciated, more-than-half-wild little bay mare quickly rose to the top of my list of associates.

Bon-Bon (yes, the name finally caught on) was my first experience with bonding with a horse and, in hindsight, she taught me much about the secret language and psychology of equine. Years later, long after I'd made plenty of human pals and my sisters and I had graduated to showing registered Quarter Horses, my admiration still went out to that wise little mare who never let a locked gate or high fence keep her from grazing the neighbor's pasture or "cavorting" with the local stallions. Bon-Bon taught me a lot about exercising will and intention to get what you want in life. It was great fun to watch her in action.

I like to tell people that horses can help humans to learn a few things really well—leadership, sensitivity, and boundaries are three good ones—but I'm highly doubtful that you can learn about true friendship from a horse. Many of us anthropomorphize the bond we have with our horse, claiming that it surpasses that with our human friends, our family members, or even our spouses. But we are mixing apples and oranges. We believe that our horse is giving us unconditional *agape* love when—at best—our horse is treating us like a fellow herd member, subject to domination and at the mercy of the abundance or scarcity of resources.

Rather than a true friendship, taking on ownership of a horse is more like adopting a small child. You will need to be responsible for that horse's wellbeing and education. You will need to ensure the horse knows basic manners and is developed into—and remains—a safe and productive horse, be that for riding, driving, or even just for therapy. I like to imagine that the next owner of any one of my horses is someone's precious young granddaughter (perhaps even my own). What kind of horse would I want to hand over to her? What kind of ground manners and behavior under saddle would I like to encourage in the animal, and what behaviors would it be my ethical duty to discourage, if not eradicate?

This is where I might trot out some ghastly stories of people who taught their horses to grab carrots from their mouths, only to have the horse bite off someone's nose at a later point in his life. One of the girls I rode with as a teenager had taught her horse to buck when she touched a certain part of his back by offering a reinforcing food reward for that behavior. Such a trick might impress your friends, and it is great fun if you're a skilled rider and prepared for it. Unfortunately, the next unwitting owner of that horse may have paid the consequences.

So, what is the difference between a friend and a herdmate? Friends forgive and overlook each other's weaknesses. Herdmates take full advantage of weaknesses, even probing and testing a bit to see where they are. ("Boo! Oh, did I scare ya? Not gonna eat that hay after all? Here, allow me to clean it up for you.") In essence, herdmates are the equivalent of "frenemies."

Herdmates vote for their herd leader every day, and adjust their own status accordingly. That accounts for most of the fighting and sniping that goes on in herds of horses. Especially in feral groups, the greatest thrill in the world for a horse is catching a fellow herdmate sleeping in the sun and successfully chasing them off their spot. In that moment, running off the other horse has raised one horse's status above another's; quite literally he stole the other's real estate.

This is where people often get confused about their horse's behavior toward them. As they spend more time together, the human begins to develop tender feelings for the animal, the beginnings of what feels like a love bond. However, the more time the horse spends with his human, the more he may look for ways to play his game of dominance... even if it's just balking on the way to the arena (introvert) or mugging pockets for yummy-smelling treats (most extraverts). A herdmate that is of higher status would never tolerate being touched by another horse without an express invitation. What looks like friendly behavior—rubbing his head on your shoulder, for instance—has its roots in dominance and may eventually escalate to more aggressive displays.

Now, before I come off like some grumpy spoilsport, let me explain the concept of becoming your horse's B.O.S.S. (beneficent and omnipotent source of supply) and why I think it's a better goal than mere friendship. First of all, beneficent means generous or good; omnipotent means having ultimate power and influence; source refers to a person from which all things come; and supply means provision. Not to put too fine a point on it, the B.O.S.S. of the herd is the generous and all-powerful provider of all good things. Let's go over what those things might include for a horse, and how we might prove to the horse that we are indeed its source for all good things.

Safety

Remember the hierarchy of needs? This is the bottom rung, which means it is the most basic need for a horse. Safety doesn't have to do with providing shelter and a nice blanket to wear. It is more of an attitude, which leads to actions that demonstrate protective leadership. Remember how I protected my herd of two mares by chasing the goats? This is how we impact our bond with our horse, by saying, "I'm going to chase away from us any potential threat."

Here is an exercise you can accomplish today when you go to the stable to see your horse, assuming there are other horses nearby: Take your horse out to where there is a fence with loose horses behind it. Lead your horse along the fence and see if the loose horses come up to investigate. Keeping your horse a safe distance away, swing the end of the lead rope toward the horses and reinforce the message to stay away with your body. If the horses aren't persuaded to move away, hit the ground with an overhand swing of the rope. Under no circumstances should you actually strike the other horse and do let the owner of that horse—or anyone else observing—know what you are going to do beforehand, to avoid any misunderstanding. The idea is to move the horse away even just a few feet, as a gesture of protection toward your own horse.

Comfort

This level of the needs offers many opportunities to show beneficence and omnipotence. The lead mare would address the herd's survival by locating good places to graze and good sources of water. When the wind is bitterly cold, she might lead them into a dense tree grove or between rock outcroppings. If you keep your own horses, you are already seen as the source of food and water, but what can you do if you board?

Simply taking your horse out to a grassy area and spending time letting him graze can move you considerably higher in status and is a better choice than just showing up with treats every time you visit the stable. Another idea: See if you can work out a deal with the stable owner for him to put your horse's feed outside the pen on the days when you're with your horse. Then, you can be the one to "provide" his dinner meal.

I once rescued a Mustang mare that had been starved badly and hadn't been handled much in the years since she was bought at a BLM auction. I knew we would need to have a vet look at her promptly, so I decided to escalate the bonding process. I placed her in my round pen, with no immediate neighbors or companions. For two weeks, I brought her meals out to her and then would sit with her while she ate. In addition, I only put enough water in her stall to fill a feed bucket and I emptied the bucket when I left. Soon, she began to whinny to me when she saw me approach her pen. We weren't *friends*, per se, and I still had a struggle on my hands to get a halter on her, but she was beginning to recognize my usefulness and to look forward to my showing up, feeding her, and offering her companionship.

A year later this mare had become a solid trail horse that I'd named "Sage." Although she still wasn't very "user friendly," she and I had an understanding born of that early bonding work. All too soon there came a time when I would sit with her again, this time as she lay writhing on the tarmac outside the veterinary clinic. She was in advanced stages of a severe colic; the scarring created from years of parasite infestation had created a twist in her intestines.

At one point, Sage rolled her head onto my lap and gave me an unmistakable look that said "Do it...now!" Then I told the vet waiting nearby to give her the shot that would relieve all pain forever. Does a friend make that call on a friend? I don't know, but a B.O.S.S. does.

Companionship

Here is another area where a human can make a significant impact on their horse. However, it does require a time commitment. As I mentioned earlier in the "Five Signs You May Have a Bonding Problem" list, you can't defer an appointment with your horse for too long. Eventually, the horse will bond, probably with its neighbors, and will begin to exhibit reluctance to go away from the comfort and security of the stable; he will become what we call "barn sour."

At my ranch, I play musical stalls with the seven equines, switching them from run-ins, to pasture, to dry lot, and I mix and match them with different neighbors. Even so, allegiances and preferences develop. For instance, everyone wants to be my lead mare's grazing mate and hardly anyone likes to be stabled with Travis (or as we like to call him, "Mr. Grumpy"). Again, if you are boarding at a commercial stable, you may not have the ability to switch stalls. In such a case, putting in longer hours with your horse is all the more critical. The best idea of all, though, is to haul your horse on a multi-day trip, preferably for a couple of weeks. When removed from the normal social scene of his stable, your horse will learn to rely on your companionship. Even if it's a case of "any port in a storm," you are getting that horse's attention and your B.O.S.S. skills have a prime opportunity to manifest.

Play/Dominance
"Be wary of the horse with a sense of humor"—Pam Brown

Horses don't have senses of humor like we do. They don't guffaw at the standup comedy routines on television, or think of themselves as witty and urbane (although one of my mares does seem to have a droll wit). Their playfulness is connected to their exuberance and their endeavors to improve their social status. While it is a joy to watch horses at play—especially wild horses— a horse that persists in wanting to play rearing and biting games with humans is a potential hazard. Remember that someone's granddaughter may eventually get hold of this horse and so helping him learn to control his exuberance when in hand or under saddle is a critical part of his training. I take a tip from my alpha mare, Nikki, who doesn't allow any exuberant behavior from the other horses within a ten-foot radius...her personal bubble. If they come close when they're kicking up their heels, she screams and drives them away to a respectful distance.

The Case for Prey-Predator Bonding

Do animals love or bond cross-species, as *we* understand the concept? I have been trying to answer a philosophical question regarding animal consciousness and how they perceive each other, based on an experience I had a few years back.

Rio, a two-year-old gelding I'd had since he was a baby, showed signs of "wantin' to get sick," as we in the horse world describe it—fever, nasal discharge, little appetite. So I called the vet, who arrived, took the colt's vitals, stood back and studied him, and finally agreed that he looked like he was "wantin' to get sick." The main concern with a fever is that it dehydrates a horse, which can lead to complications like impaction colic when not enough moisture gets into the intestines. So, the vet loaded him up intravenously with antibiotics and hydrating fluids (at about a thousand dollars a quart, gauging by the bill I got later).

I was standing in the barn aisle and watching the vet truck pull away, with my colt's head still cradled in my arms, when I had the sensation of being watched myself. I looked around and there were my two Dobermans, the three barn cats, and an errant chicken that flat out refused to stay in the coop. They were fanned out in an almost perfect semicircle around the colt and me. The animals were watching us with such intentness and, well, peacefulness that it prickled my skin. It seemed that all species represented in that barn aisle were bonded together, prey and predator alike, in a moment of communion with the colt. (Okay, in retrospect the chicken may have been scratching for food a bit but I'm giving her credit anyway, just for being there at the right time and hitting her mark.) Relating this story is about as "cosmic" as I'm going to get in this book, but the experience has caused me to be more open to what these occasions of prey-predator harmony may signify for all of us on the planet.

Top Ten Things You Should Do With Your New Horse in the First 30 Days

1. Quarantine or isolate him from other horses for at least 10 days, if possible.

2. Contact his breed registry and update his ownership papers.

3. Have your farrier assess his feet.

4. Bring him up to date on any vaccinations.

5. Assess his body condition and map out a nutrition plan for improvement, if necessary.

6. Make sure your existing tack fits, especially the saddle, and modify or replace as needed.

7. Consider micro chipping if you are in a high horse traffic area, i.e., boarding at a large boarding complex or fairground.

8. Spend an ENTIRE day with your horse, getting him used to your sight, smell, sound, and feel.

9. Work on trailer loading skills, if necessary.

10. Consider giving him a more meaningful, appropriate—or just fun—stable name.

Chapter 4: "Hey, That's My Spine You're Sitting On!" The Connection between Comfort and Behavior

"The behavior of horses—or perhaps we should say the misbehavior—often reflects the behavior of the person handling or riding the horse." —Dr. Robert Miller

"The truth of the matter is, horses seldom develop problems on their own."—Mark Rashid

Because I believe in full disclosure, I'm going to take you back to a time before I learned some of the natural bonding skills I cover in this book. The year was 2003, the second war in Iraq was about to begin, and I was having my own skirmishes with a young horse named Rio San Bravo.

His Peppy San-bred American Quarter Horse sire had come off the old John Wayne estate in northern Arizona, which is by way of explaining his name. Although I'd raised him from a weanling, life events had gotten in the way of my developing a strong bond with the colt. In short, he'd languished in my stable from the age of one until I finally decided to send him for some professional training at nearly three years of age.

Rio's personality was of the "puppy dog" variety and I thought I'd put a good handle on him before sending him out for sixty days of professional training. However, the horse that returned shocked and scared me. He had become a thug, resorting to dominating threats and intimidation to get the upper hand, on the ground, in the round pen, and under saddle.

Of course, I now know this was to cover the great fear and pain that had been instilled in him by the less-than-sensitive, good-ol'-boy, rope-em-choke-em cowboy trainer I'd sent him to. Sure, I'd heard of natural horsemanship and even been exposed to a little bit, but I was just sending the colt out for some saddle training, right? What was the big deal?

As it turned out, how you start a colt is a big, big deal. That is why so many natural horsemanship clinicians teach colt starting these days. The value of having built a bond through learning a common language really begins to make sense when you put a saddle on a horse's back for the first time.

There is one thing worse than a horse with no training and that is a horse with a very bad attitude toward training. I knew I needed to find a direction to go with Rio, and that is how I ended up at a press junket week on natural horsemanship. I sat in a circle of other journalists in the dining room of the training center the first night. When my turn came to tell what I hoped to get from the week, I stammered on about Rio, who I'd brought along in search of a fix.

"There's this horse I have...and...he's about ten seconds away...from having my number."

It was hard for me to express to a roomful of strangers that I was all out of ideas on how to get through to the big red dun. I knew there was a component missing from our relationship and that it was up to me to seek it out. My young gelding was proving increasingly dangerous to work with, both on the ground and under saddle. After spending most of my life taking my early horsemanship skills for granted, it felt embarrassing to say I'd met my match.

There was general tittering in the group over my initial use of humor, but thankfully the clinician, his wife, and several staff members took me seriously. I got plenty of support and some fresh ideas that week, but more importantly, committing to learning a more natural way of horsemanship gave my rude rogue of a gelding a second chance at a happy life.

The following was an editorial I wrote just a scant eight weeks before I took the first step toward natural horsemanship that would lead Rio and me on the path to a more useful and less stressful way of relating. It's important for you to know just how far I had to come to join the "natural" discussion.

Choose Your Battles – (April, 2003)

The impending warfare in Iraq must have been on my mind as I tacked up Rio to do some trail training with my riding coach, Shannon. Lately, my 16-hand, 1250-pound gelding has been a bit too exuberant outside the arena, especially in the first mile of road we take to get to the trailhead. Since it is during that time that we pass by the majority of riding obstacles—loud barking dogs, trailer trucks, railroad tracks, trains on said railroad tracks, "monster" water towers—it makes for a nerve-wracking journey. Okay, I admit it—I'm wimped!

So far, Rio has done all the scary stuff, oh yeah—jump, whirl, buck, rear, buck-and-rear-simultaneously and—most ominous of all—this mincing collected jig that makes me feel like I'm straddling a medicine ball about 20 feet off the ground, followed by some more bronc riding. I know it's my age talking—actually screaming in my ear that I need a safer horse—but I've decided to just make this horse safer to ride. So, enter Shannon...

As she eyes the whip and spurs I am assembling in the tack room—my arsenal—I hear her clearing her throat and imagine her contemplating how to broach the subject of pacifism.

Shannon: "You know, Rio's not so bad once you get him down the road a piece."

Me: "Yup, that's true (fiddling with the straps on my spurs). It's getting him there that's the key."

Shannon: "Why...don't...we, uh, leave those aids behind and just see what he does?

—Whoaaa! Screech! Let's stop right there while I tell you about Rio's "bad boy" predecessor, a gelding of similar weight and stature named "Goodman"...

I had bought Goodman as a very, very "green broke" three-year-old about a dozen years earlier. He was possibly not the ideal pleasure mount for the mom of a young child, whose health and paycheck were depended on but hey, the price was right.

A sabino paint chestnut with a flaxen mane and tail, Goodman had all the charisma of a rock star—combined with the instincts of a mafia hit man. I had wrongly assumed I could finish his training by simply employing my award-winning show equitation as we moseyed down the trail...

The first time Goodman bucked me off, just a scant week or two after I'd bought him, I was so shocked that my self-preservation didn't kick in right away. I simply stood up and got right back on—a knee-jerk response instilled in me by countless movie cowboys. Nothing had changed for Goodman except that the "nuisance" was climbing back onboard and now appeared mentally loaded for bear. Sure enough, from that time on, the "nuisance" never mounted up without her spurs strapped on and whip in hand. War had broken out and neither side was taking prisoners.

This was a departure for me. A product of the genteel horse show rings, where I put my sweet Western Pleasure show ponies through their paces in front of scrutinizing judges, I'd never ridden with spurs as weapons and had usually carried a whip on trail rides to flick off insects or discourage sneaky grazers.

Now, each time I felt Goodman bunch up, duck his head, raise it to the stars, or do all three, I'd grab one rein and wrap him into the equine equivalent of a cinnamon roll. I'd heard somewhere that a horse couldn't be in that position and buck you off. Then I'd flail on him with my outside aids until we'd done about a dozen really fast whirls and he was begging me to just stand still and let the world stop spinning. There he'd stand, licking his lips—I presumed his version of saying "uncle"—and peace would once again reign on the trail. I'm not proud of what I did to achieve that peace, but it did give me the confidence I needed to ride this horse.

Eventually, Goodman did come to respect the upper hand I had and would "behave," just as long as I continued to bring along my riding aids. Of course, the days invariably came when I would forget to strap them on, possibly hoping the gelding had outgrown his wild ways. On those rides, his antics simply returned with a vengeance.

Back in the present, Shannon is pleading her case.

Shannon: "I think we should NOT make a big deal of Rio's behavior to begin with. Let's just see what he's really wanting to do."

Me: "Ummm..." Clearly, he was wanting to smear me all over the road.

Shannon: "Ride him in a balanced way, weight centered, and keep that slight lateral bend in his neck to let him know you're in control and he needs to listen."

Whaaat—no cinnamon roll? No whirling dervish? No easy fixes that would lull me into a false sense of security? Not in the least. It turns out, riding is a trust partnership between horse and rider, and if ever there was a time to start building trust, it is in preparation for first ride out of the arena.

So, Shannon and I have agreed to start our trail rides in the arena, where Rio is usually so mentally torpid it's a wonder he doesn't just curl up and take a nap. With the gate open, I mount him and make a few laps on the rail, then proceed out of the arena. As soon as he's outside, the gelding's energy level rises dramatically and I can feel him get "happy feet," so back we go into the arena for a few more laps.

Shannon and I hope that eventually, Rio will take this calmer, more subdued behavior down the road and out onto the trail. In the meantime, I'll lay down my weapons and learn to ride the horse I have...

Goodman was eventually helped by a gifted equine chiropractor, who diagnosed bursitis in his hip, possibly caused by rearing over backwards with his previous owner. The saddle I was using on him was causing him to experience intermittent spasms of pain, to which his response was to try and rid himself of both saddle and rider. After several treatments and a better-fitting saddle, Goodman became an excellent and steady trail horse, and eventually we even competed in some distance races.

Rio, my big red dun gelding, eventually moved on to a loving forever home in California—a natural horsemanship home, of course!—and while I regret his rocky start as a colt, I will ever be grateful that he was the horse who sent me in search of better and more natural solutions.

To what extent does comfort, or lack of it, affect behavior in your horse and get in the way of successful bonding? Well, since it comes in only behind safety in basic needs, don't be surprised if a physical discomfort, sometimes created and often aggravated by a piece of tack, is getting in the way of forming a strong bond with your horse. As we saw with Goodman, it can make a horse dangerously impulsive. However, it can also have the opposite effect.

Since horses are extremely sensitive to stress and discomfort in their bodies, chronic pain can cause them to detach from sensation, leading to a generally dull response to a rider's leg and rein pressure. You can find this behavior in any rental horse string, where life for the horse largely consists of moving from Point A to Point B, then back to Point A with as little exertion as possible. Long ago, these horses learned to ignore their "dude's" dubious, confusing, and sometimes painful rein and leg cues in order to save their jobs and their sanity.

A Natural, Sensible Approach to Teeth and Hoof Care

Another source of pain for a horse can be the mouth and teeth. Veterinary knowledge of the role that tooth and mouth pain plays in horse behavior has grown exponentially since my rodeo days with Goodman, some twenty years ago. Since a horse's teeth are designed to grow continually throughout his lifetime, the slightest bite abnormality—often due to unnatural feeding practices—can create painfully sharp points, shelves, and edges in his mouth. Left untreated, dental problems can turn a mild-mannered kid's horse into a fire-breathing bully. Conversely, as with tack that inflicts chronic discomfort, mouth pain can cause a horse to shut down and act depressed (not to mention, drool a lot!) Best solution? Yearly mouth checks with your regular vet or an equine dentist. However, if you even suspect there might be a problem with your new horse's mouth, don't wait for the check-up.

Telltale symptoms of mouth pain can include:

- Weight loss
- Resistance to being bridled
- Spookiness or unusual reactivity in situations
- Resistance to drinking, especially drinking cold water
- Picky eater and spits out food
- Often shakes head when eating
- Bad odor to the breath
- Discharge from a nostril
- Drooling
- Excessive yawning

- Swollen jaw (in the case of extremely neglected teeth where an abscess has occurred).

A few years ago I would have urged you to seek out an equine dentist exclusively, but many more vets have recognized the need to educate themselves beyond just the eight or so hours of instruction on "teeth floating" that they received back in veterinary school. That said, I do suggest that you arrange to be present when your horse's teeth are worked on (you are his advocate, after all) and that you work with your vet to avoid or minimize the following practices:

Excessive use of drugs – If your horse must be sedated (and that is often the reason I'll choose a vet over an equine dentist who is not licensed to administer sedation) make sure the vet starts with the least amount necessary. You can cut down on the amount of meds by working with your horse's mouth to desensitize him to the process of palpating his back teeth. Just be careful not to get bitten!

Overly forceful restraints – I direct the vet tech not to "ear" my horses—the process of grabbing an ear to hold the horse still—as it can make them quite head shy and is counterproductive to all the work I've put into making them easy for my younger students to halter and bridle. It's just as effective to hold the halter as it is a sensitive body part and if it comes down to a choice, I would rather sedate than use undue force.

"Hanging" the horse to elevate its head – This only happened once on my watch, but I've been vigilant about it ever since. The vet apparently had a bad back, so his tech rigged an overhead pulley and hoisted the sedated horse's head higher in the air, where it was easier to work on. Since this a completely unnatural and potentially damaging position for a horse, especially one who has head and neck issues to begin with, I would again advocate for a more humane solution.

Power grinders or Dremel tools: These items have become popular due to their convenience for the operator. But for a horse with jaw problems, such as TMJ (temporal mandibular joint) disorder, the vibration from the tool can be excruciating.

I once drove around northern Arizona with equine dentist James Ford for the day while we were writing an article together. Of the 15 to 20 horses he examined and worked on that day, not one of them required sedation. At one stop I assisted by holding out my hand to collect a full set of baby teeth that popped right off a young palomino mare, who spent most of the time docilely leaning into Jim. While not all areas of the country enjoy the services of equine dentists, more qualified technicians are emerging all the time, especially those who base their work on the principles of "natural balance." I certainly urge you to look into their availability.

In Support of the Hoof

Feet are another issue that may come between a new owner and his horse. To shoe, or not to shoe... Actually, my stance is that the horse should stay the way he came for at least a few months before making any significant changes to his feet. The exception to this is the rescue horse, whose feet have been neglected and are in immediate need of attention.

Such was the case with Sage, the mustang mare I rescued. Sage had toes so overgrown and misshapen they curled up like elves' feet. The day my farrier was scheduled to come and make some sense out of her poor feet I couldn't get out of a work meeting, so I left a check and a note saying simply "Do what you can to help her." Imagine my surprise when I arrived home just as he was putting away his tools and he took me by the arm over to where she stood docilely in her pen. Nearly glaring at me, he picked up one of her feet to show me the sole.

"You see this?" he said, indicating the immaculately trimmed hoof. I did, noting that a hoof of near perfect proportions had been lurking under all of that growth. "That is a one-inch hoof wall—I measured it. This girl will be able to climb boulders barefoot... Don't you DARE ever ask me to put shoes on her!" And I never did.

Other horses have not been so well endowed. A Paint gelding came to me for boarding, purchased by a girl who was new to horses but had been impressed by an equestrian friend's barefoot philosophy. So, off came her new horse's shoes and within months he had developed a quarter crack due to uneven pressure on his significantly deformed coffin bone, as x-rays later revealed. What exacerbated that problem was the girl asking a farrier who was not schooled in natural trimming technique to pull the shoes. The farrier gave her horse a "pasture trim," which may be great for riding in lush pastures but offers a horse little support and protection from Arizona's lava rock terrain. The girl was so anxious to take charge of the horse's care that, rather than wait to consult a natural hoof care expert in the area, she forged ahead with a trim that cost her plenty in vet bills and downtime as the quarter crack was treated and slowly grew out. Fitting the horse with some hoof boots for riding on roads and trails would have been a good intermediary step in turning a shod horse into a barefoot one.

The Bonding Value of Nursing an Injured Horse

While helping a horse recover from injury isn't high on anyone's wish list, it can be turned into an opportunity for bonding, especially with a new or rescued horse. If you are seen by the horse as the one who provides relief, the one who knows how to ease the pain and help the horse feel better, you may find the seeds of a bonding relationship take root.

Of course, the farriers and veterinarians who are called into service will urge us all to put a "handle" on a new horse as soon as possible, thereby making their job of treating and rehabbing safer and more successful. This means making sure your new horse knows how to stand nicely for the vet, and how to pick up his hoof and stand nicely on his other three for the farrier. Failure to do so could jeopardize the life of the professional, and will definitely have a direct effect on how soon they will return your call to schedule the next visit. While I always try to accomplish these goals with a new horse, sometimes life conspires against me. Take the case of poor Twinkle, the Premarin filly I adopted at just six months old.

I hadn't quite gotten the little filly used to haltering when she had a mysterious accident in her stall one night that resulted in my discovery of a deep gash on her front leg the next morning. A long strip of flesh had been carved from just below her knee to the front of her fetlock joint. It was oozing dark blood and showing some white tendon. I speed-dialed the vet and went back to wait with the filly. I could tell she was depressed and shock-y, as she didn't make me chase her all around the pen to get her halter on.

I hadn't even named her, at that point. She was just a rescue from a group of four hundred Premarin foals that had been destined for the feedlot. Someone had super-glued a piece of cloth with the designation "A-14" on her rump.

For the uninitiated, Premarin stands for "pregnant mare's urine," an elegant name for the substance used to make hormone replacement therapy (HRT) treatments for menopausal women. Developed in the late 1940s, Premarin became the most popular HRT on the market. At its peak, upwards of 35,000 mares per year were giving birth to mostly unwanted foals—by-products, really—in Canada and the northern Midwest region of the U.S. A number of horse rescues became involved in finding homes for these foals, often contracting directly with the Premarin ranches.

Sometime around the beginning of this millennium, researchers evaluated results of a very large study on nurses taking horse-derived estrogen products and realized the subjects placed on Premarin were at greater risk for heart problems and certain types of cancer than the control groups. The researchers discontinued the trial and almost overnight the Premarin industry folded in on itself. This meant that the filly known as A-

14 was one of the last large generations of Premarin foals, and for that I'm grateful.

Now A-14 was glaring at me with incriminating eyes, as if somehow I had snuck down during the night with a carving knife and filleted her shin.

"Nonsense," I told her. "I was up sleeping in my bed. You did this to yourself!"

I did feel cross with myself for having put shavings in her stall, instead of out in the pen where it would have been safer for her to lie down and roll. In reality, anything new or different—including a location change—increases the risk of injury for a horse, according to "Mr. Murphy" and his laws... I hated to think I had caused this filly to travel across half a continent only to damage herself at her final destination through my own poor judgment. What I didn't know was that this incident would mark the beginning of our bond... the start of our growing into heartmates.

The vet arrived, cleaned the wound, and wrapped it like a mummy, but not without several tussles and some strong opinions shared.

- No, she didn't want her leg shaved with that noisy, buzzing thingy.
- No, she didn't like the look of those metal scissors that were cutting the flap of skin on her shin.
- ...And she'd had just about enough of sharp things poking her in the neck, butt, and leg!

That next night, exhausted and in the midst of needing her to stand still for only the second of a ten-day course of antibiotic shots, I drew the filly—now named Twinkle—close to me and murmured soothingly in her ear that if she would just hold still for a moment I would never let her down...she'd see...life would get better, be better with me. She drew a deep breath, exhaled, licked her lips, and let me give her the shot. Things eventually did get better and she has pretty much trusted me from that day forward.

Top 10 Questions You Might Ask a Seller Before You Buy a Horse

1. How long have you owned the horse?

2. Where did the horse come from?

3. Has he had professional training? If so by whom?

4. Who rides him now, and how often?

5. Where do you ride him most often? (i.e., arena, ridden to trails, trailered to trails)

6. Has he ever been turned out with a group of horses? If so, how was he?

7. How is he for the farrier?

8. How can I access his current veterinarian and vet records?

9. Is there the possibility of a trial lease before I purchase?

10. Is there a money back guarantee?

Chapter 5: Rider Confidence: A Missing Ingredient in Successful Bonding

"It is not enough for a man to know how to ride, he must know how to fall"—Mexican proverb

"There is no disgrace in getting off a horse and getting a hold of his mind." –Ned Leigh

We all want to think that our nerve and equestrian potential are as limitless as they were when we were twelve. However, the real world has a way of acquainting us with our physical and mental frailties, not to mention responsibilities to our jobs and families. Those obligations require us to take precautions to avoid damaging ourselves. Thus, we ride with a certain level of risk awareness that uses fear as its alarm system.

Nearly all riders, regardless of riding level, will come off a horse at some time or other. A fall from a horse, or even a scary near-fall, can seriously affect the bond between human and horse, particularly if it comes in the first few months of new ownership. In this section, I'm going to talk about a few riding mishaps, not to scare you but to illustrate what the rider can do to build back confidence in themselves as well as in their horses.

Ron, a 50-year-old seasoned distance rider, was riding home alone from a practice ride when his mare tripped over a rock and went down. "Actually, we were walking down a slight grade and when she stumbled, we did a slow somersault," he told me ruefully. He ended up in the hospital with a broken pelvis, a fractured wrist, and a slight concussion sustained when his mare rolled on him.

Months later, when I ran into him in the feed store, he still had a slight limp and was beginning to deal with his fear of getting back on his mare and starting trail training again.

"I'd never been seriously hurt riding before this," Ron explained. "It came as a real shock how casually it can happen. I mean, we were walking home—not racing! I developed a phobia of the whole accident site" This was unfortunate, as it was right at the entrance to the park where he rode.

I asked Ron what he was doing to help overcome his fear. Because he had to go through a lot of physical therapy and healing, he took advantage of the time away from riding to join a gym and build his body back up. Soon, he began hiking the trail where the accident had occurred. Finally, he started leading his mare past the site. (Fortunately, she had sustained no injuries). One day, after a few weeks of hiking together, they had just passed the scene of the crash and were at the entrance to the park. Suddenly Ron felt a surge of confidence; he got on his mare and rode the whole trail system before heading home.

"On the way home, we passed by the crash location and I could feel my adrenaline surge. Peaches, my mare, seemed really affected too." More likely, he had communicated his anxiety to her through his leg and rein aids. "She got so antsy that I started to talk to her and to slow down my own breathing to control my fear. I think it was focusing on the horse, knowing she trusted me and was mirroring my response that helped me get over it. We both wanted to survive to ride another day!"

I checked in with Ron recently and he has resumed his conditioning rides. At first, he could only get past the crash site by focusing on controlled, steady breathing and keeping his eyes on the trail ahead. Now, he barely notices where the spot is when he passes by. Hours of confident, fun, positive riding have replaced the memories of what happened to him on the day of the accident.

Ron is my hero.

Few people, including me, would feel strong enough to take such a straightforward approach to dealing with the residual feelings that get in the way of fully coming back from a riding accident, i.e.,

- Getting strong and healthy again.
- Desensitizing yourself to the circumstances (location, horse, etc.) associated with the accident.
- Practicing mindfulness and intention regarding riding into the future. You can't change what is past but you can change how you feel about it.

Instead of doing that, however, we often tend to blame our horse, our companions, the equipment, even the weather. ("My horse gets spooked on windy days"... "I need a stronger bit"... "Their horses were out of control, which sent my horse off.") We suspend all equestrian activities until we've found horses, equipment, friends or climate conditions that are more favorable to our wellbeing.

Even when our minds are willing to let bygones pass, our bodies remember the pain. When this happens, our subconscious mind can take over, in the interest of self-preservation, and will sabotage any enthusiasm we might have for spending time in the saddle. The tack room suddenly seems in disarray and needing a thorough cleaning; the horse is just possibly the tiniest bit lame on his left hind; or we don't want to be late for that root canal appointment we made. Before we know it, another month has gone by with minimal visits to the stables, let alone any substantial riding time.

Another friend of mine, Katherine, bought a five-year-old Thoroughbred who had recently made the transition from slow racehorse to recycled pleasure mount. Although she hadn't had any accidents or even near misses when I talked to her, Kat's great fear was that she wouldn't be able to stop Killian if he took off with her on the trail, which had already happened more than once.

"He's very forward on the bit, which I love in the dressage arena, but it scares me on the trail with all that impulsion and energy," she explained.

At least Kat was savvy enough to know that switching to a more severe bit would just compound her problems. For a horse that is impulsive and likes to move his feet, being held on a tight rein can create a claustrophobic feeling similar to being trapped in a trailer. A better solution would be for a rider to do bending and circling patterns, asking for specific movements instead of restraining all movement.

Kat knew she shouldn't head out on the trails alone, but bringing others along brought out even more energy in her gelding and served to increase her fear. Eventually, I convinced Kat to find a mount more suitable to her skill set and temperament. By selecting the attractive and charismatic Killian in the first place, Kat had chosen her "own poison," as Pat Parelli likes to put it. This refers to a rider's tendency to "over-mount" or "miss-mount" themselves with a horse that needs a much more skilled and assertive rider. An impulsive horse—either from fear or play drive—will eventually get the best of a timid, inexperienced rider. Such an unfortunate choice can destroy a rider's confidence and enthusiasm for horses, if not hurt her outright.

This doesn't happen just to new riders. In fact, Kat had studied dressage for years but had always ridden horses that were more tractable and wasn't used to putting out the mental and physical effort her young ex-racehorse demanded.

"I had to re-evaluate my priorities and opt for safety over the thrill of riding a more spirited, showy horse," Kat told me. "It wasn't easy because I had bonded with Killian, who's just a love with great ground manners. I also had a lot of pride invested in being an 'expert' rider and looking good on a big strapping courser."

Another friend, Pat, who found herself in the same predicament of being over-mounted bought a second, more seasoned horse to bridge the gap between her current skill level and the expertise her first horse choice required. For those who can afford this solution, bringing in a more seasoned horse has the added benefit of giving the more impulsive horse a nice, calm buddy on the trail. Pat is an educator and she described her situation in academic terms.

"I bought a young, green horse that was at the graduate level when in reality I was barely out of grammar school," she said with chagrin. "Luckily, Poco came along and she's been an excellent tutor."

Pat rides the older mare on the trail and takes arena lessons on the "graduate student." Having two horses is twice the financial and time commitment, but Pat feels that riding the older mare has given her greater confidence and made her a better rider in half the time it would have taken with just the green horse. To help keep costs down, Pat is planning to half-lease one or both the horses to an excellent young rider she knows, which will also ensure they get sufficient exercise between her stable visits.

Sometimes a fall off a horse can result in fear and anxiety that approach clinical levels. Sandy really thought she might never get over the accident that left her with a plate in her right ankle. She and her parents had invested a fortune in the Warmblood mare she was riding at the time. After some introspection, Sandy realized that it wasn't falling off her horse that frightened her; it was fear of hitting the ground! This new fear of gravity was creating paralyzing fear in her and making it impossible to get back in the saddle. Sandy had danced when she was younger, so she decided to go back to class and learn how to fall.

"Then, when I felt that I'd mastered the art of landing fairly safely," Sandy told me, "Gravity wasn't this big scary force anymore."

For many other riders, the solution has been learning the emergency dismount. Even riders who have never had a fall report feeling more confident with the emergency dismount under their belt. They feel much more empowered over all the possibilities that can take their mind hostage.

Whether a rider's fear is based on flying (losing control of your horse), falling (hitting the ground and injuring yourself) or a little of both, the anxiety and phobic feelings such fear creates is bound to register with their horse. And no trust bond can occur when the horse is picking up that the supposed leader of his herd is breathing shallowly, clawing at the reins, and entertaining negative thoughts.

In fact, more than one rider has said to me, "It seems like every horse I get on wants to spook out on the trail." *That is because the same fear message is going out from the rider and each new mount is interpreting that message as, "There's something scary in the bushes."*

Sadly, a large percentage of the people who get into horses get back out within a year, deciding it's not the sport for them. I'd venture to guess most of those people simply got hold of the wrong horse for their skill level. Clearly, making sure the horse you choose is a good match with your experience and temperament is the overriding tip for enjoying equestrian activities and staying safe. Just as people who are compatible with each other find it easier to form a satisfying relationship, a horse and rider who are on the same wavelength will have a better chance of forming that much desired trust bond.

Top Five Ideas to Help Improve Rider Confidence

#1.   Focus on breathing. Practice breathing deeply and slowly; count up to ten each on the inhalation and exhalation. This will help you relax and slow down your racing pulse. If it proves too nerve-wracking to concentrate on, chew gum; somehow that helps with breathing and stress reduction.

#2.   Develop a repertoire of soothing songs, preferably lullabies, and SING to your horse. I sing old show tunes, not because I'm a big fan of musical theater, but those were the songs my mother sang to me and singing them instantly relaxes me. If you absolutely can't sing, whistle or hum the tune instead. I've heard it said that horses respond well to music, but maybe they just like being around people who respond well to music.

#3.   Use creative visualization. Some equestrians use guided or unguided imagery to help create the ideal riding scenario—i.e. visualizing the horse perfectly under control and the rider feeling strong and capable—which they can focus on to get them through rough patches while on board. Others use imagery to create what-if scenarios and then work out the particulars for themselves and their horses. For instance, "If my horse grabs the bit in his mouth and takes off, I'm going to bend his head around, set my arm against my leg, and not release until he comes to a complete stop."

#4.   Wear protection. If you have read the list this far, make sure you've also purchased and are wearing safety equipment, such as a helmet and maybe even a vest. I'm not going to go into a long spiel on the whys and wherefores of helmet wearing (hint: As an ARIA-certified riding instructor, I'm a huge advocate for helmets) but I do know that a rider's confidence goes up when she's taken responsible steps in the direction of her own safety.

#5. Invest in riding lessons, if necessary, to develop an independent seat. The more secure you are in the saddle, the more able you are to ride out the jumps, bumps, swerves, and stumbles that might occur any time you are on horseback.

Perfecting Your "Pre-flight Check: Ten Things to Do Before You Get on Any Horse

Some of these suggestions might be hard to negotiate, especially with a "dude" or rental horse, but not impossible. Ask the horse's owner if you can just work with the horse on the ground for a while prior to getting on. Even if you only accomplish a few items on the list, you will have moved that much closer to ensuring a safe ride.

1. Take a few moments to connect with the horse. This can be as simple as finding an itchy spot and giving it a good, satisfying scratch. Horses will do this for each other in pasture and they don't ask for nearly as much cooperation as we riders do.

2. Make sure you have proper riding gear, including a helmet. If you are skeptical about the value of safety headgear please visit www.extension.org/pages/Demonstrations_of_Falls

3. Inspect the horse's feet for any rocks, debris, loose or missing shoes, or cracked hooves.

4. Take a walk around the riding area and check for rocks or debris that might injure the horse (or you, should you dismount quickly).

5. Inspect the tack—including making sure the saddle's cinch or girth is in good shape and tight enough, and that the headstall, reins, and chin strap fit properly and show no signs of weakness.

6. Observe the horse's movement and facial expression. Don't get on a horse that is obviously agitated without knowing what is causing the agitation.

7. While still dismounted, make sure the horse can go over a two-foot obstacle without discomfort. If he can't jump it or refuses, there may be a saddle fit or lameness issue that needs checking out before you mount up.

8. Make sure the horse will respond to rein pressure: If possible, attach a lead rope of at least 10 feet to his bridle and wrap it around his rump (on the opposite side of where you are). Then see if he will "unwrap" himself by following the pull of the rope and walking in a tight circle. Does he bend his neck or brace it? How well he responds to this will predict how well he responds to the feel of rein pressure.

9. Check for a horse's responsiveness to your leg by applying pressure to his side with your hand or fingers, on his barrel just behind the stirrup. Notice how much pressure you need to move him sideways a few steps.

10. If you have access to it, check the horse's response to a plastic shopping bag tied to a stick or riding crop. You would be amazed at how often a loose Wal-Mart bag on the trail or in the arena can ruin an otherwise enjoyable ride.

Chapter 6: There Are No Bombproof Horses

"Your horse can only be as brave as you are."—Unknown

"All horses deserve, at least once in their lives, to be loved by a little girl."—Unknown

The term *bombproof* has come to mean any horse that would be suitable as a child's or beginner's mount. Actually, the label was first applied in a military setting, back when the cavalry division actually rode horses. It probably stopped being an accurate description around the time tanks replaced horses on the battlefield.

Apart from horses that are rigorously trained and used by mounted police officers for patrol work, few horses on the market these days have been exposed to bomb explosions. Such a cacophony of sound, mixed with the vibration of the impact would send any half-alive horse running for his life.

When people place ads to sell their "bombproof" horses, at best they are telling you, "I've found this horse to be safe, calm and happy in his present environment." What they cannot tell you is whether the horse will stay safe, calm and happy in the next home he goes to. That will depend on a number of factors, including his innate personality and temperament and how well he adapts to the new situation. And *that* will depend on whether he feels secure, is reasonably comfortable, and is a good fit with the existing herd (including the human herd).

Regarding suitable mounts for children, many people think ponies are an automatic fit. While their size may be appropriate, their temperaments and spirit levels may not. For example, ten-year-old Shawna begged her parents to get her a horse when her family made the move from Chicago to Arizona. Her mom was surfing on the Internet when she ran across a picture of an adorable pony named Copper. The parents bought Copper long distance and had her shipped out west. Indeed, she is the most adorably petite, pinto pony who happens to be a talented jumper with tons of energy—definitely not a rank beginner's trail mount! The last I checked, Copper had thrown Shawna off five times in four months. Recently, her mom put the pony back up for sale, saying Shawna isn't really interested in horseback riding anymore. A family of natural athletes, they had just assumed that riding would be one more sport they could enjoy together without any instruction or guidance. Sadly, many people who are improperly mounted as Shawna was quickly lose interest in the sport and some develop a lifelong fear of horses and horseback riding.

One of the consequences of choosing a pony over a horse is that your children will outgrow the smaller animal just as surely as they outgrow their shoes and clothing. With any luck, a child-friendly pony will be passed along from one loving home to the next, giving a succession of children their first joy of horse ownership. When my son was five, however, a pony came into our lives that would put a new spin on this notion.

Her name was "Bandy," short for abandoned, which she most certainly had been. Dumped off a truck into a barren oil field in Fillmore, California, she was little more than a battered skeleton with no food, little water, and a scant desire to keep on living. Some people across the road watched the pony standing motionless in that field for the better part of a week before they got it in their heads to call someone.

At the humane society, volunteer vets gave Bandy a 50-50 survival chance, all the while pumping her full of fluids and antibiotics, smearing her wounds with salves, and taking a "wait and see" approach. But a lone farrier, working on the pony's cracked and overgrown hooves, sensed the heart of a fighter pumping deep within her frail chest. The farrier started appearing daily with an astonishing array of groceries for the pony. Equally astonishing was the rate at which the little animal made them disappear.

After the two-week limit was up for her to be at the Society, the farrier took the pony in and started making calls. When one is looking for a suitable mount for a child, word gets around. Before long, my son John and I were strolling down to the farrier's paddock to "look a gift horse in the mouth."

Let me stop a moment and address some of the issues in the last paragraph as they relate to choosing a mount. First, rescued and emaciated horses are not always the best choice for a new rider. As their body condition improves with better nutrition, so may their temperament change or—more accurately—begin to finally emerge. Second, as I've already stated, a "suitable mount" does not necessarily need to come in a pint size. In fact, the smaller the horse is the more headstrong and feisty he may be. In the wild, this fierce determination may be what keeps him alive. Third, a free "gift horse" may come with considerable baggage— from lameness to behavioral problems to use restrictions—all of which need to be factored into the equation. You may end up spending more on maintenance with a free horse than you would with a horse you purchased.

The first time I laid eyes on Bandy, tears rushed into them. She was without a doubt the ugliest pony I had ever seen. Her head was three sizes too big for her emaciated frame, her backbone loomed like a small mountain range, and her angular rump seemed borrowed from some miniature bovine. An unevenly shedding coat seemed to start with a base color of brown, over which a maddened graffiti artist had gone wild with silver and white paint. Standing straight up and out from her body and going from black, to white, and back to black again, her mane and tail gave Bandy all the gravitas of a Mattel toy. Finally, white hairs ringed her pink eyes, heightening the suspicious stare with which she regarded all things in her world. Dreamy childhood images of a sweet and corpulent Shetland pony faded from my brain as Bandy cast me a sullen look and moved to a distant corner of the paddock.

"She's a bit shy of people but won't put up too much fuss about being caught," the farrier told us. The phrase "Too weak to resist" crossed my mind as I watched her amble in slow motion around the corral, her mouth just inches above the ground. And so, just four weeks after her rescue from the "field of horror," we took Bandy into our care.

At the feed store, I watched with misgivings as the cash register total climbed into the triple digits. Free pony, my you-know-what, I muttered as I opened the back of my SUV and loaded in about four cubic feet of grain, supplements, and medications.

To her credit, the little girl could eat. In all the time we had her, I never once saw her turn down a morsel of food. In fact, once her own portion was consumed, it was a never-ending source of amusement for us to watch her commandeer whatever food her pasture mate couldn't gobble down in time. Raising herself up to her full eleven hands, Bandy would scream so loud and so high, it was a wonder that packs of dogs didn't instantly appear from all directions. There was never any fight. With the noise she made and the skill with which she maneuvered her hind end at him the Arab gelding she shared space with could do little more than flee in terror.

I had no tack for a pony, but finally manage to locate a pony-sized shocking pink nylon bridle with a diminutive curb bit and took my son for his first ride on his very own pony. As we climbed a small hill in the pasture, I looked back just in time to see John slowly siding off Bandy's rump, accompanied by many tufts of shedding hair onto which he had been desperately grasping. In the quiet of the breaths he drew between howls, I explained that he was now just two spills away from "bein' a real cowboy." He and Bandy both stared back at me in hostile disbelief as I announced he would need to get right back on for the spill to count.

Sadly, the day eventually came when I realized that my son was not going to be the young horse lover I had been and had hoped he might become. By this time, after over a year in residence with us, Bandy had grown into an athletic and robust firebrand, a shining example of her Pony of the Americas breeding. Her energy and drive far exceeded my child's endurance and abilities. Ever more frequently, we were returning from trail rides exhausted—John physically and me emotionally—from trying to keep the pony controlled and the rider safe. It was clear that our little girl needed a home with a child better suited to Bandy's emerging powerhouse personality.

I put an ad in the local paper and turned down a few dozen phone callers who were looking for a quiet "bomb proof" and "dead broke" pony. Not Bandy, I politely told them, and felt like adding that there was one down on Main Street outside the market if they had two quarters. Finally, a suitable home appeared and I arranged to bring Bandy over for a 30-day trial lease. I had great hopes, as my ad had caught the eye of a woman with three young daughters who had Pony Club experience and wanted to compete in gymkhana events. Of course—gymkhana! Racing around barrels and poles would be a perfect fit for an energetic, athletic pony. I drew up the lease papers, faxed them to the woman, and waited for the weekend, I would take Bandy to what I hoped was a forever home.

The night before she was to leave, I let myself into Bandy's paddock, armed with a carrot. I had done this nightly for the past year and a half. The treat usually bought me time for a furtive hug of the stout neck and the opportunity to bury my face for a moment in that Mattel-made mane. In my heart, I knew I was saying goodbye to more than just my son's pony. Bandy had become the dream horse I would have wanted at his age.

Normally, my drawing close to her made the little mare nervous and she would always move away to a safe distance. Tonight, however she stood still for my embrace long after the carrot had disappeared. Her stillness seemed to hug me back and say, "It's okay, Mrs. Jackson, don't cry. I just outgrew you is all."

Top Five Potentially Best Horse Breeds* for Beginning Equestrians

1. Quarter Horse (Retired, foundation bred)
2. Paint (Retired, QH foundation bred)
3. Draft-QH cross
4. Gaited (i.e., Missouri Fox Trotter, Icelandic)
5. Morgan (retired, trained)

* I cannot publish this list without adding a HUGE advisory about "breed buying." Basically, there are good and bad beginner mounts in every horse breed. The components that create a good beginner's horse have been and continue to be disposition, training, and age. Some of the best horses I ever rode were "Heinz 57" or *grade* horses, and I really can't cite a reliable source for those without saying, mind they don't hit your head when they fall down from heaven.

Top Five Most Problematic* Horses for Beginners

1. BLM Mustang (untrained)
2. Thoroughbred (off the track)
3. Arabian (untrained or off the track)
4. Horse bought off the Internet (and shipped sight unseen)*
5. Horse bought at Auction*

*Very GENERALLY speaking. Again, I hesitated about this list as I've personally done both #4 and #5. However, in neither case were the horses meant for beginning owner/riders. My advice is and will remain NOT to buy young, "green," or untrained horses if you are a novice rider and first time owner.

Chapter 7: Assessing a New Horse with "Follow Me"

"Every movement you make tells your horse something, either about what you expect from him or about the kind of person you are." —Jessica Jahiel

"The horse lends you his strength, speed and grace, which are greater than yours. For your part you give him your guidance, intelligence and understanding, which are greater than his. Together you can achieve a richness that alone neither can." —Lucy Rees

So, you have answered an ad for what sounds like the perfect horse for you. The price is right, the size and age seem appropriate, and most importantly, both the level of training and amount of experience seem to complement your needs. You have visited the horse and been impressed with the way he performed on the ground and under saddle in his present location. How can you go that extra distance to find out more about the horse's personality and temperament?

I would suggest arranging to lease the horse for 15 to 30 days at the facility where you will be keeping him to see how he takes to a new environment. During that short time, it will be your job to check this horse for warning signs—such as displaying a high degree of thresholds (See Chapter 2) which indicates a horse that likes to worry and doesn't have much confidence.

Other warning signs would be a horse that is antisocial to other horses, or even to people—who reacts badly to people coming into his stall or to horses approaching his pen. This would indicate a horse with poor social skills and low tolerance to pressure, which may limit the environments in which he would be safe to ride. This is also a time to get a thorough vet examination and even have your farrier weigh in on any hoof abnormalities that could foretell future soundness issues.

There is a little round pen exercise that will help give you a good idea of how a horse responds to pressure, and how easy or difficult it is for him to give up his agenda in favor of a human's. I like to employ it when assessing a horse's temperament for use in horsemanship instruction or in my therapy herd. It is apparently based on the type of sorting out that a feral lead mare will do if herd member expresses dissent. The idea is to put a degree of sustained pressure on the horse and then release it to see if the horse will come under her leadership and...follow. Done right, meaning cleanly and with intention, this exercise can shorten the time it takes for your horse to start looking to you for leadership.

The "Follow Me" Exercise

Turn the horse loose in the pen and allow him to roam around until the exercise begins. Place yourself in the center of the round pen, making sure you have brought with you a lariat, a longe whip, or a lead rope long enough to reach the horse. When you are ready to begin, turn to face the horse, lifting your lariat hand toward the horse's rump to put pressure on him to move forward. Keep the pressure on and direct the horse until he is moving along the rail in a counterclockwise direction at a consistent fast trot or lope.

After a few laps of the pen, some horses will begin to turn their heads toward you to "ask" if it's okay to slow down, to protest the pressure (toss their head at you), or even to voluntarily slow down, speeding back up only when you have reapplied the pressure. The horse needs to move around the circle three or four times on his own, keeping at least a trot going. Once this has occurred, drop the lariat or whip and start to walk around the pen in a *clockwise* direction, close enough to the rail that you will pass within touching distance of the horse as he comes around. Don't stop or even look at the horse as you pass, but continue walking around the pen with intention, meaning with your eyes focused on something ahead of you. Once you are past, peek back and see what the horse has done with the release of pressure. A horse that is used to tuning into his human will probably turn and want to follow you. Allow him to catch up and walk shoulder to shoulder with you. Try out some left or right turns as you walk and see if the horse will stay up with these direction changes. How readily the horse changes direction with you will correlate to how focused and grounded you are combined with how desirous of comfort he is. I try to dole out comfort with rubs and scratches while we're walking as soon as I see the horse trying to give me what I'm asking for in the way of partnership. After all, comfort is another need that a B.O.S.S. supplies. It may take sending the horse off to the left a few times to trigger his comfort seeking behavior.

On the other hand, you may find some horses will not seek to connect with you, even after sending them around the pen numerous times. Horses that are withdrawn from humans, for whatever reason, may have made some unfavorable decisions about such contact. This could be due to their innate nature or to a history of abuse. Typically, they will wander off in a different direction, drop their head and start scouting for food, or they may just keep running in the direction they were going, refusing to adjust to the release of pressure from you.

Here are some typical responses I've found to this round pen exercise:

1. A black and white Paint gelding, whose age is "20-something," does a faster walk around the pen in response to your repeated commands to move out at a faster gait. You finally manage to get him trotting, but he frequently stops to look at you quizzically. Without continued pressure on him, he'll just come on into the middle and hang out with you, lowering his head so you can scratch his ears. If you finally do get him to keep his trot going for a few times around and then walk past him clockwise, he falls right in step with you and seems happiest "dogging" you in this way. Congratulations, you have found yourself a "beginner" or child's horse.

An older horse may be harder to motivate to really move out in this exercise, depending on his soundness and disposition. Only in this situation would the term "bombproof" appropriately describe the horse's detachment from life in general. In fact, many older horses—say ages 22 and above—are perfectly wonderful baby-sitters and beginner horses. Just don't expect them to rise to the challenge if and when your riding tastes get bolder and you find you want to do gymkhana or barrel racing. That is where we got the term "starter" horse.

2. A young Arabian mare that you are looking to purchase is quiet and responsive to your pressure, travels well, and looks very alert and engaged in the round pen. Yet when you drop the lariat and turn to walk clockwise, the mare slows as you pass, then stops and turns to look at you. Will she join you in walking around the pen? Not really... Instead, she very pointedly turns and wanders off the other way to stand gazing back at the barn where the other horses are hanging out. This tells you that she is very social and discriminating. You have not yet impressed her as

worthy of her attention, let alone of following docilely around the circle.

Mares are often very hard to win over with this bonding technique, particularly if they rank highly in their own herd. An alpha, or lead mare, often feels she should be the one doing the schooling, not some human. She would have to virtually abdicate her throne to be willing to follow you around. Horses that are both quiet and dominating can fool a lot of people into thinking they are good for beginners. While they can be for the right human personality, they can also outsmart their owner and easily get the upper hand in the relationship. Though not impossible, it often takes a lot of knowledge, focus and personal fortitude, to win over such a horse. Unless she is approaching old age, has an extremely kind personality, or you are working with a coach or trainer, she could prove too dominant and wily for a first horse.

3. Another young mare gives you bursts of impulsive energy in the round pen, with the slightest gesture of your lariat. Some of her favorite actions include dramatically switching directions, kicking up her heels, often in your direction, and giving you the "stink eye" when you do put on pressure with the lariat. On the plus side, she is just plain beautiful and you could watch her move all day. She also requires very little effort to motivate. When you drop the lariat and start the counter walk, she is very happy to connect with you and keeps up with your every direction change.

However, she does come with some minuses. She has a strong play drive and likes to make up her own games or put spins on yours. Unless she has had the kind of thorough, systematic training that a professional employs, including ground work and finished bridle horse work, the exuberance she demonstrates may come back to haunt you when you're under saddle. That's because this is the kind of horse that doesn't often tolerate mistakes made by a learner. While her energy and athleticism is not always the best choice for a beginning rider, such a horse temperament combined with a solid training foundation would make her a good choice for someone who is working with a trainer toward a specific performance goal, such as reining or dressage. The trade-off is, while you get more horse at first and must take measures to stay safe, you also get a competitive horse that you will not outgrow and have to say goodbye to after only a couple of years of riding.

There are plenty of other responses to this round pen test, all of which can give a potential new owner a better idea of where that horse is on the hierarchy of needs, his tractability, and reaction to applied pressure.

"Test Driving" a Prospect

Two examples from my own horse buying experiences come to mind. In each case, I was looking for a well-trained horse that would pack a child or beginner. When I went to test out Nikki, my Andalusian-cross mare, I brought along my son John, then a strapping nine-year-old, to help me assess her suitability. We arrived in the late afternoon and found that the horses at the stable had just been fed. The owner pulled Nikki away from a full manger of food, tacked her up, and then showed us to the riding area, an enormous open tract of BLM land. I simply got on the mare and rode off from the stable. Although she did emit what I took to be small grunts of protest, she moved out easily and had a soft, responsive mouth.

Nikki felt light and responsive from the very first moment I mounted her. All of her gaits were accessible with just slight pressure. When I brought her back, I was pretty sure I wanted her, but needed to see how she would ride under a child's hand. I looked around for some enclosure where my son could ride her. The mare seemed calm and gentle enough but I didn't want to take chances with my son's wellbeing. I found a larger paddock that would work and watched as John guided her around the enclosure.

I ended up taking Nikki based on her temperament...she hadn't known me "from Adam," but was willing to leave her food and her herd to ride out into the high desert with me. She had also handled just as easily for a child with minimal riding experience. Those are huge pluses in any horse. That was 18 years ago and she is still the horse I teach beginners and children on. She has developed a fan club of student riders over the years and I've had several offers to buy her.

In contrast, I found my Quarter Horse gelding, Travalena Chex (Travis, for short) in the midst of a weeklong shopping trip for an intermediate lesson horse. On my to-see list were several professionally trained; retired show horses. This subgroup of horses is an excellent, but often overlooked, source of beginners' mounts. People often don't consider such a horse because they think they'll end up spending a fortune. On the contrary, horses that are at the end of their performance careers are well trained, well traveled, and often modestly priced to ensure a good retirement home. Travis' owner was desperate to sell him quickly and to a knowledgeable home. Given his talent and training, his final selling price was ridiculously low. However, the point of this story isn't what he cost, it's how successfully he hid his true personality from me in the buying process.

When we arrived at the boarding stable where Travis was kept, his owner already had him saddled and was riding him in the arena. He was a pretty mahogany bay, but quite overweight, having languished in a small pen for at least a year. I noticed his owner was wearing roweled Western spurs and riding him in a high-port curb. These are the accoutrements of a reining horse rider, and it turned out that was Travis' previous "occupation." Not only that, he was from a line of distinguished Quarter Horse performance horses, including King Fritz and Travalena.

In the arena, the owner showed him off on the rail at all gaits and then hopped off and handed me the reins. Riding Travis was like getting into a Mercedes Benz AMG coupe. He was compact and nimble, with excellent lateral movement and collection. He knew exactly where all four of his feet were at any given moment, and still does—although these days he reserves his greatest nimbleness for handily backing out through a maze of buckets, grain sacks and detritus in the feed room without touching a single thing on the rare occasion I've forgotten to secure the lock! In short, Travis seemed so much like the perfect horse I'd been searching for in my riding instruction business that I felt I didn't need to put him through any more paces. That's right. No personality assessment. No trail ride. Just ordered up the standard vet check and returned with a check and a trailer.

The day I got him home, the gelding's real personality began to emerge. He was food aggressive. He didn't bond well—with people *or,* it appeared, with other horses. He chased everyone away from his stall, especially small inquisitive dogs. In the round pen, he galloped and galloped in a circle, but even after a half hour of running refused to even glance in my direction, let alone ask if he could stop or come in. He did not allow his face or body touched without being haltered first. Once haltered, he became quite reactive to pressure, backing away at the slightest movement of the lead rope and, when I asked him to come in to me by pulling on his lead line, coming close and turning sideways as if to say "Here, get on and stop all this other nonsense." In short, Travis had learned to be obedient and compliant under saddle while remaining otherwise fearful and detached from humans.

Normally, detachment would not be that big a problem. After all, it's the fate of a lesson horse to be ridden by numerous students within the course of a day. In a way, it helps to have a horse that is not very opinionated about who is riding him, i.e. a horse that has a forgiving nature and the patience to tolerate the kinds of mistakes that beginning riders make.

Some horses, like my mare Nikki, handle multiple riders with great confidence and generosity of spirit. She learned long ago to trust that she would be treated well in all cases, that I "had her back." When a horse behaves like Travis, it is partly because of his innate temperament—sensitive and on the hot side—and a great deal because of how he has been trained and handled.

Around the time I got Travis, I was in transition from teaching just straight riding and horsemanship to working from a more therapeutic and experiential model. My group of lesson horses was transitioning into a therapy herd. They were required individually and as a group to be loose in an arena and interact with my human clients, following the EAGALA (Equine Assisted Growth and Learning Association) model. That was something Travis had never done before... just moving at liberty in an arena and interacting with one or more humans on the ground. The first few times we tried him in the herd, it did not go particularly well for him or us.

To be fair, the only frame of reference he had was the western performance sport of cutting cattle. In this event, the rider guides the horse into a herd of cattle and separates one cow from the pack. Typically, a horse's ears flatten as he jumps at the cow to keep it from rejoining its buddies and he can look downright scary. This is precisely what Travis did to a Native American boy who had been tasked with haltering him. As the boy approached, Travis lunged at him with his ears back. My spiny senses made me lurch forward as well, preparing to run interference.

The boy stepped back, temporarily daunted but not discouraged from his objective. Mindful of the experiential learning aspect of the work, I held back to see what choices the two would make next.

The minute the boy had retreated, Travis' ears had pricked forward as if mentally lifting a hoof in the air and shouting "Score!" The boy approached again and Travis again jumped at him, but this time the boy stood perfectly still. Confused, Travis' ears came forward again. In the silence, the boy walked up and put the halter on him; he and the gelding worked together without incident for the rest of the session.

Since that first session, Travis has come a long way in learning about the at-liberty games and activities that we play. He is still prone to put on an aggressive demeanor, which works particularly well with our juvenile probation groups. Yet, he has also learned to play "Follow Me" in the round pen. In fact, he is my secret weapon; having picked up on the mechanics of the exercise like a dancer learns choreography, Travis knows the exact moment when he should peel off and follow the human.

If I have an insecure student or client, I'll pair them up with Travis in the round pen and he will nearly always turn and follow them at the end of the exercise. It is an instant confidence builder for the human. However, true to the sentient nature of the horse, even Travis will mirror back half-hearted or uncommitted attempts. Clients soon learn that the horse will meet them in the middle, but cannot be expected to do all the work.

A horse with Travis' quirks might not be a good horse for someone new to horses and planning to keep him at home. His food aggression is a huge defense mechanism. When he snakes his neck and gives me the "stink eye" I simply tell him, "Knock it off—if I had wanted your food I wouldn't have given it to you in the first place!" However, his behavior might intimidate someone with less experience. He has certainly fooled more than one stall cleaner with his aggressive mugging.

Because Travis has never offered to bite or kick anyone—his scary act is just that, an act—I continue to use him in a selection of the at-liberty activities. However, since not all horses are "more bark than bite" (or should I say "more whinny than kick"), being exposed to this behavioral outlier could mislead a newcomer into disregarding critical warning signs from another horse.

Whoa Nellie vs. Speedy Gonzales

Another good way to find out about the horse you are planning to buy is to determine whether you have a "Whoa Nellie"—a horse who continually has a foot on the brake—or a "Speedy Gonzales"—a horse who likes to idle at warp speed. These distinctions can be part of their temperament, but can also be due to their previous occupation. For instance, there seem to be few Thoroughbred ex-racehorses who are Whoa Nellies; the ones that are probably have some sort of soundness issue.

Running is the purpose both of their breeding and of their training. The same can be said generally about Arabians. They were historically bred for distance racing under extreme desert conditions, so if you are going to ride an Arab, pack nutritious snacks and plenty of water; your endurance *will* be tested. While some breeding programs have produced bulkier, more substantive Arabs that are used for arena work, the innate nature of these beautiful creatures is still to move their feet first and think about it later. I mention these two breeds because of their prevalence in the horse market (along with the ever popular Paint and Quarter Horse). Personally, I wouldn't endorse a Thoroughbred off the track as a good horse for a beginning rider, unless the animal was quite old and had traded in his "track shoes" for a pipe and some slippers.

I have known Arabians that squeaked by as a beginner or child's mount. The qualifying individuals had other attributes, such as professional training and a large degree of experience that made them safe under normal circumstances. (I'm also taking into consideration their unique history with humans: Sheiks kept them in their tents, raised them on dates and camel's milk, and generally accepted them as family members.) However, they are considered hot-blooded and are apt to get "happy feet" when they become fearful, insecure, or excited.

Whoa Nellies can occur in any breed, but the most extreme examples would be found in horses that are the polar opposite of the Thoroughbred and Arabian, i.e., the cold-blooded draft breeds. Most draft breeds originated in northern Europe around the time humans first discovered the benefits of horse labor and transportation. Traditionally used for farm work, purebred draft breeds such as the Shire, Suffolk, Belgian, Percheron, and Clydesdale don't usually find their way into recreational riding circles. Bred to be slow and steady, they are textbook Whoa Nellies. However, the more popular draft/Thoroughbred crosses, referred to as Warmbloods or sport horses, often retain the mellow draft disposition while displaying the greater athleticism of the light horse breeds.

There is another kind of Whoa Nellie, which I described in the round pen scenarios. This horse *can* move, but just isn't sufficiently motivated to do so. The beginner who takes on such a horse must learn to differentiate between "I can't move forward because I'm frozen with fear" and "I won't move forward because I don't see the point in it and after all, I don't really believe you can make me." The former is a threshold issue (see Chapter Two) and the latter is a dominance game.

Dominance can be a threshold of sorts, communicating, "I know more than you do about what's best for me," but it is also a powerful call to action. When a horse is trying to control the situation by balking, it requires you to do something that will demonstrate to that horse that you are a capable and resourceful leader. It is a "pop quiz" for which you need to be prepared with answers on the spot. To back down or release the pressure on a horse that is bracing or pushing back is to teach that horse that such behavior will reap benefits; you can expect to see more balking in the future.

Leadership with a horse is best established before the saddle goes on. One technique that you can employ to demonstrate ground leadership is to turn your horse loose in the round pen or arena and allow his attention to wander off. When he is off in his own world, simply walk around to stand several feet away from his hind end and, if the horse still ignores you, lightly flick him on the backside with the end of your lead rope. The idea is to surprise the horse, but not to inflict pain or discomfort. If he is truly surprised, he will probably jump forward. Don't chase him. Just calmly walk in a semi-circle to the opposite side of his hindquarters, wait to be ignored, and flick again. If the horse now tracks you and turns to face you, try giving the command to move forward. Many times this is all it takes to get a Whoa Nellie unstuck and moving his feet. Eventually, just a tilt of your head and a glance back at the horse's hindquarters will be the cue for a horse to move forward, either toward where you stand in the center of the pen, or in any direction you are asking.

Licking and Chewing Moments

Learning to recognize the differences between fear and dominance and to do the right thing at the right time to address the behavior will raise your value in your horse's eyes. Remember the first time someone said just the right thing to you at a critical point in your life, called you on your "stuff" and you suddenly thought: "My gosh, this person is on the ball! He really understands me!" In the horse world, we call that a "licking and chewing" moment.

In response to your refining when and how you put pressure on the horse, you may see licking, chewing, and head shaking as the endorphins release in the horse and he begins to feel calmer. The moment when he starts to lick his lips with his tongue, you may also see his jaws open in a multiple yawns. These are signs of a shift going on in his state of mind, a general lessening of anxiety. If he happens to be focused on you at that moment—for instance, during the "Follow Me" game in the round pen—he is probably updating something about the way he experiences you and his environment, which is causing him to lower his anxiety level.

The good news is that you are there to allow him to make that shift and enhance this new, relaxed state of mind. By hand grooming or massaging his back or finding that special itchy place, you are demonstrating that you are the beneficent and omnipotent source of supply—the B.O.S.S.—who can help keep him safe and comfortable, and provide an abundant amount of companionship and interesting recreation.

Epilogue: Bonding With an Aging Horse...

"Yet when the books have been read and reread, it boils down to the horse, his human companion, and what goes on between them."—Walter Farley

Most people who own horses will have the experience of knowing that horse through its youth and into its prime. Some of us will then have the pleasure of owning the horse into its golden years. In the case of my Andalusian-Arabian mare, Nikki, our "dance" has lasted nearly 20 years.

She came into my life as a powerfully charismatic, yet sweet and gentle seven-year-old. Back then, her morph toward gray had just begun; she sported an ebony mane and tail, and deep gunmetal dapples were erupting through the copper remnants of her bay base coat. Today, she is the color of snow, the flea-bitten flecks of brown all but hidden by her heavy winter coat.

The first time I noticed any age-related difference in Nikki's behavior was several years ago on a large trail ride I was hired to help outfit. Although my friend Sharon and I had about 20 horses at our disposal, we also had each brought along our "ace in the hole" horse to make sure there would be a sufficient number of gentle mounts. We put a young woman with little riding experience on Nikki and set her at the front of the line; I was supremely confident that my gentle alpha mare could act as "point horse" while my partner rode in the middle of the pack and I rode "drag."

Imagine my chagrin when, five minutes into the ride, I heard a familiar trumpeting neigh and saw Nikki starting to prance sideways down the trail like a parade horse. I couldn't think what had quickly turned my 23-year-old seasoned pro into a bag of nerves. We had the line of riders halt as I rode up to where Nikki was pawing the ground with agitation. I had the rider dismount and I put her on the calm horse I had been riding. I took hold of Nikki's reins and pulled her aside so the line could move forward. She instantly stopped moving her feet and blew out a long sigh, licking her lips. Then I mounted and we picked up the tail end of the line with no further incidents.

For the remainder of the two-hour ride, I mulled over what had happened. It seemed like the mare had had a lapse in confidence; she was in an unfamiliar environment, with a strange rider, and none of the horses around her were in her "herd." Although I had loaned her out to other riders plenty of times when she was younger, I had done so with less frequency in the last few years. Perhaps she had lost some of her "seasoning" in the past five years and had slowly begun to slip in confidence. The vital young mare who had boldly traveled out from her stable on the day I "test drove" her was not the same today. In the past years, her dark grey dapples had faded to a flea-bitten white and her eyes had taken on a less focused, more vulnerable look. All at once, I realized I had an aged horse on my hands.

It was a profound a revelation as looking into a mirror and seeing signs of my own aging. Not that Nikki was ready to retire from being ridden, and certainly not from teaching beginners in the comfort of her own arena. She was simply manifesting some of the limitations we all discover as we age—the eyesight weakens, the joints get achy, and most importantly, our reliance on our social supports becomes more critical. On the ride that day, I had been her only social support—her token herd member—and she had been calling me to her out of her need for security.

Almost two decades earlier, as a new horse in my barn, Nikki would often quietly and confidently second-guess the decisions I made as her B.O.S.S. It took me at least six months to get her to stop "schooling" the other horses when I rode her on trail rides. Most frustrating of all was her insistence on a direction when we came across forks in the trail. She seemed to have an inner sense of correctness—no doubt her innate instinct as lead mare—and it was often at odds with my agenda. While this made her wonderfully steady with beginning riders, it was challenging for the more advanced rider.

Somewhere over the years, Nikki and I succeeded in forming a bond, despite the fact that she was the "guest horse" I always loaned out to insecure riders. I remember coming home from more than one group trail ride astride a more fractious mount while its rider enjoyed the even temperament and smooth gaits of the gentle grey mare. There is a reason I labeled her "Serenity" on my website.

The final phase of our relationship developed through the equine-assisted work that we do. When I first turned the horses out loose in the arena and had clients come in to do activities with them, Nikki had amused herself by playing "catch-me-if-you-can" with many a hapless client. She would dash around, nudging the others to move their feet and thereby inciting a stampede. After about ten minutes, she would then tire out and stand docilely while the people approached. Visitors were always amazed when told that she was over two decades old!

Lately, I've detected another shift in our relationship. Maybe it's that the dashing around is too tiring, or that she's just bored with it, but now when I first bring people into the arena, the grey mare sidles up to my side as I discuss safety around horses. More often than not, when I brainstorm about how to keep safe around a horse, Nikki has positioned herself so that I can easily walk around her body and point out areas. In other words, she has appointed herself my demonstration model and stands perfectly still without restraint as a parade of participants walk around her from one side to the other with their hands on her.

Being my "model horse" somehow causes her to lick and chew at the very moment I discuss the meaning of licking and chewing, a phenomenon that several people have pointed out to me in different sessions. It also means that I can no longer count on the usual oppositional behavior horses demonstrate in a herd when people try to coerce them over or through obstacles—an experiential learning aspect of the equine-assisted work. Once Nikki sees that they have constructed a jump, she simply runs over and jumps it at the start of the exercise. Thus, an activity that we planned to take 25 minutes, with lots of opportunity for processing failures, exploring group dynamics, and facilitating team building, takes roughly 90 seconds when Nikki is the chosen horse.

Does the fact that she irons out much of the inherent conflict in the activities and that she now relies on me to orient her to her surroundings frustrate me or make her less valuable in my eyes? Not in the least. It endears her to me. It shows me that Nikki has learned to trust me and to go with my ideas, even when I'm counting on her to have her own! After all this time, Nikki has finally voted for me as her leader—her B.O.S.S.—and for that I am eternally grateful.

Bonnie Ebsen Jackson is available for consultations, coaching, and clinics designed to help new owners and their horses become safer and happier in their relationships. You can reach her with inquiries and feedback at t.h.e.ranch@mac.com.

CPSIA information can be obtained at www.ICGtesting.com
Printed in the USA
BVOW011911150212

283044BV00001B/7/P